The Photography of Women

THE NUDE AS ART

LEWIS TULCHIN

The Photography of Women

WITH PHOTOGRAPHS BY THE AUTHOR

A. S. BARNES & COMPANY, INC., NEW YORK

THOMAS YOSELOFF LTD., LONDON

© 1964 by A. S. Barnes and Company, Inc.

Library of Congress Catalog Number: 64-15385

A. S. Barnes and Company, Inc.

South Brunswick

New Jersey

Thomas Yoseloff Ltd

18 Charing Cross Road

London W.C.2, England

Second Printing, 1965

6160

Printed in the United States of America

The established rules and methods of composition in art do not always apply to the photography of the human form. . . . Depicting the human figure is essentially a matter of arranging its elements in a plastic and plausible manner. . . . Compositional treatment of a still-life, a seascape, or a landscape is limited by the immovable nature of the subject, but with the human form, we must arrange the line and mass pattern of the figure to form a pantomime of motion, intended motion, or restful inactivity.

L. T.

Contents

Foreword

THIS BOOK WAS WRITTEN BECAUSE I FELT THERE WAS NEED FOR A COM-prehensive treatise devoted exclusively to the photography of women, one that would provide a complete and detailed instructional program for the amateur, the student, and the professional photographer who wishes to enter or improve his work in this field.

Every pertinent phase of glamour photography has been covered, beginning with psychological concepts and ending with outdoor photography. Faces and figures, costume elements, make-up, composition, posing, facial expressions, and lighting are discussed and illustrated in a straight-forward and logical manner. I have also sought to keep the text as lucid and simple as possible, realizing that the best way for the student to assimilate knowledge of his subject, is to eliminate the non-essentials and minimize the marginal discussions.

Although great advances have been made in the field of psychology, a great deal remains to be uncovered before the subject can be regarded as a fully documented science—if indeed, psychologists ever will be able to write the last word on it. The subject, however, has been explored sufficiently to indicate that its place in the photographer's scheme of things is an important one.

I do not wish to take the stand of the self-styled psychologist or the meddling amateur who goes about analyzing women's feminine wiles, or for that matter, the photographer's masculine or esthetic feelings. Nor do I think my experience gives me the right to do so. The subject is so vast and complex that it rightfully belongs to individuals trained in the social and psychological sciences. I shall only touch upon esthetic and psychological aspects insofar as they apply to a logical and objective approach and therefore may be presumed to further this treatise.

I offer no magic formula for success in photography. Achievement, in my opinion, depends on the person who seeks it. When the student has become well versed in the subject, it will be only a beginning. Techniques alone do not make good photographs; the important thing is how intelligently techniques are applied. I hope that the reader will enjoy utilizing the material in this book as much as I enjoyed writing it.

Lewis Tulchin

1
Psychology of Glamour

GLAMOUR PHOTOGRAPHY MAY BE DEFINED AS A GRAPHIC METHOD OF GLORI-fying the feminine qualities of women. It combines the realities of physical attraction and the intangibles of what we call "esthetics." Unifying these qualities, the creative worker not only records woman's physical endowments, he also modulates and idealizes the essence of her beauty over the whole visual and emotional spectrum of her femaleness.

His pictures will stimulate a pleasing response, while the raw impact produced by the reality of the camera lens is suppressed. Stimuli are directed to the artistic and abstract appeal elicited by woman's lovely and harmonious contours.

To a great extent, visual perception is the main sense by which we receive impressions of the world around us. Its range is practically unlimited and it is suitable for abstract and esthetic considerations as well as for every-day functional uses.

Exploring this factor with an analogy, we find that, within the vivid synthesis of poetry and prose, images and descriptions of feminine beauty are primarily impressionistic meanderings which were originally derived through the medium of the writer's visual senses. And so it is with our ability to react to visual presentations in glamour photography.

The feeling in man termed his "esthetic nature" is beyond the reach of scientific experiment. In esthetics, we do not deal with tangible realities or specific psychological reactions. At best, the investigation of man's esthetic nature is haphazard.

Despite this, man continues to seek and learn of that process within him

11

whereby thought and deed are joined with emotion in an intricate pattern. In a sense, his psychology only reveals to him why he eats, why he sleeps, or why he is driven in response to his instinctive impulses. But that which is esthetic seems to elude him; the source of inspiration often remains a mystery.

Man glimpses the esthetic briefly when, from his inner self, he perceives the wonder that is woman. In her he sees something that lifts him to praise, or to create her image, not drawn from actuality, but from the well of his inspiration—the ideal upon which rests his appreciation of beauty.

Before we can discuss glamour in a photograph, we must outline the basis for the visual attraction that exists between the sexes. It is upon this basis that glamour is sustained.

Fundamentally, visual attraction between the sexes springs from forces deep within man and woman. Each is endowed with an attraction for the other. Nature, in her diversified pattern of creation, has made this attraction so all-compelling, it cannot be disregarded by the normal human being. The attraction manifests itself in a variety of expressions. Even when it is keyed to the diffuse customs hidden within our civilized society, it remains fundamentally a physical attraction.

Pursuing this evaluation, we find that the physical emphasis of woman's appeal to the opposite sex is different within various cultures. For example, in our society, conventional standards dictate the use of clothes to cover the body and the subtle use of dress, jewelry, and cosmetics to enhance it. Among some primitive peoples, it is considered neither desirable nor natural to cover the body. They often decorate the body, but not always with clothing.

Without attempting any precise or strictly logical answers, the word "beauty," as it is used in its common meaning, suggests an elusive and intangible quality describing an ethnic standard for which women customarily strive. Too often, though, the degree of perfection sought is unrealistic or can only be created by artificial means.

In fact, the evaluation of ideal beauty is usually based on the elusive physical proportions of movie stars, or else it originates in the fancies and imaginations of photographers, illustrators, art directors, or the edicts of dress designers whose goals for the average girl are practically unattainable. There is no such thing as physical perfection in one female. A symmetrical face, a full tight-breasted, yet slim figure, a narrow waistline, overly long and slender legs, and a flawless complexion are a combination of beauty assets out-of-this-world and probably belong on some distant planet—not ours.

In their efforts to adhere to a beauty standard, women resort to subterfuge; they apply make-up; they dress in a provocative manner; they use jewelry, subtle and suggestive perfumes, and other means of making themselves attractive.

The importance of being attractive is highly emphasized in our society. Many times a day, in magazines, on billboards, in store windows, and on television and motion picture screens, women are influenced by standards and techniques of physical attractiveness, propagated by high powered presentations. Women are taught to regard the photogenic features and poise of the fashion model as an indispensable yardstick of all that is alluring and captivating to man.

Of all the contemporary arts, Hollywood, and the many movie magazines that chronicle its affairs, exert a special influence on the average woman. Reaching with subtle propaganda into every town and hamlet, they have set up artificial and exaggerated standards of beauty that cannot possibly exist in reality.

As if these paradoxes were not enough, women are assisted in their quest for beauty by local beauty salons as well as modeling schools in the larger cities who, in many cases, know very little about their profession, yet impress their unsuspecting victims with articulate discourse and expressions of authority. These self-styled experts use the make-up techniques developed by the movie studios, applying them to all faces at random and often with such complete disregard for the individual woman's features, that the appeal and personality of the face is lost. Frequently, these techniques lend an artificial or mask-like appearance, with lips that are too small or too large. Eyebrows are plucked too thin, lined too heavily, or arched too much. This description may sound comical, but the tragedy of it is only too obvious.

It is inevitable that a woman's distinguishing features become objects of attraction to man, and that a well-proportioned woman is one whose physical assets are naturally endowed or artificially presented so. In either case, it is her secondary sex characteristics that are regarded by man with admiring contemplation.

The features which are most attractive to men are those physical characteristics which emphasize the dissimilarity of the sexes. These differences form the keystone of woman's attractiveness—for example, the contrast of a woman's softly curved pelvic structure and her gracefully flowing body lines and rounded flesh forms as opposed to a man's more closely knit and angular body. This in itself produces a basic ideal for attractiveness.

Among the physical traits of well-proportioned women, most men regard the hips, buttocks, and breasts as the most attractive features. The shape of these areas present the decisive structural dissimilarities of women as opposed to men (Figures 1, 2, and 3).

It is interesting to note that, in many European countries, the attractive significance of the ample and curvatious bustline is so highly prized that, although the rule against the exposure of the body is strictly enforced, women are allowed to wear low plunging necklines that show breast cleavage (Figure 4).

13

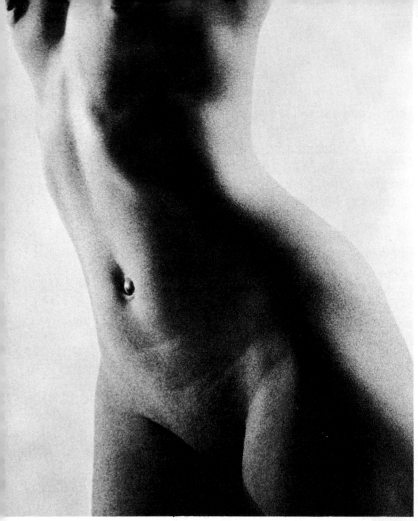

1. The Hips

2. The Buttocks

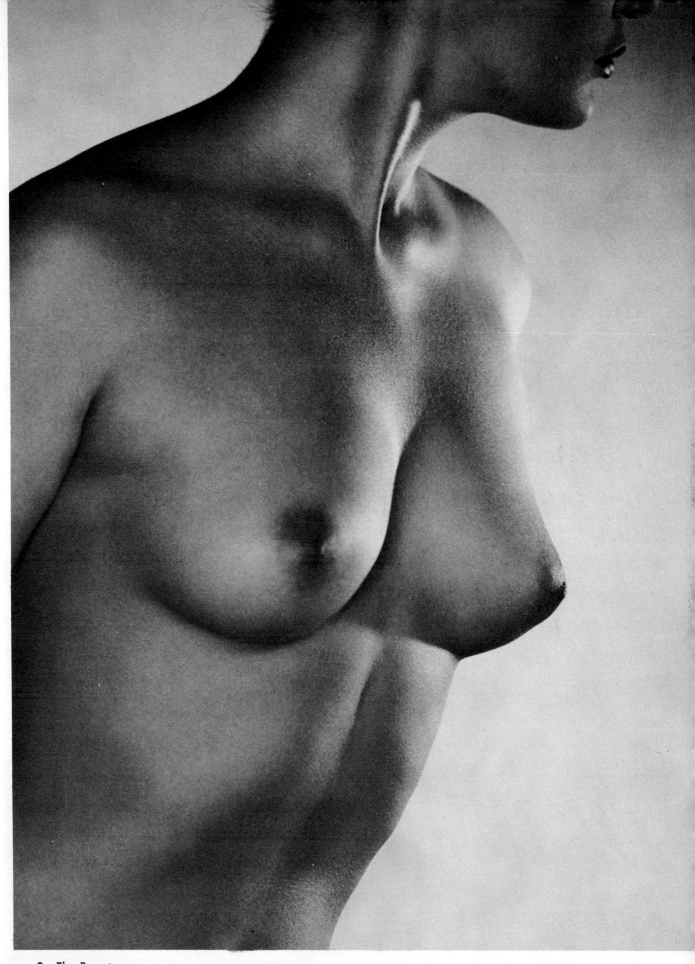

3. The Breasts

4. The Curvatious Bustline

A well-turned leg always catches the eye and pleases the senses. The impact and allure generated by attractive female limbs is best illustrated in our contemporary art. A good example is the famous "Petty Girl." Mr. Petty created a girl with overly-long streamlined legs. Although the "Petty Leg" does not exist in real life, an illusion of it can be produced with photographic techniques.

Inasmuch as the average American girl possesses long and exceptionally attractive legs, they should be considered a contributing asset to her feminine charm (Figure 5).

The flawless contours of a beautiful girl in a negligee or a man's shirt can look more provocative and radiate more appeal than if she were in the nude. The potency of a woman's charms can often be enhanced by the art of concealing and revealing her physical attributes with the use of costume elements. Thus, it leaves something to the imagination (Figures 6 and 7).

The literary phrase, "a woman's eyes are the mirror of her soul," is something that cannot be disregarded in the photography of women. As an effective and interpretive medium, a suitable facial expression adds immeasurably to the mood of the picture. Such facial expressions as a warm smile, a far-away look, a demure, coy, teasing, languid look, a submissive, wanting-to-please look, or a saucy innocent look—as if to say, "why do men look at me?" These are the facial expressions that must be included in the production of effective glamour photographs.

In Figure 8, a world of meaning can be interpreted in the projection of the girl's sex appeal. The passive reclining pose, the sensuous mouth, and the mood in her languorous eyes reveal the potency of her charm.

If we look around in our world of women, it becomes quite evident that perfect facial proportions have been given to very few of them. Despite this, women who have irregular features can be made attractive with the skillful use of make-up, applied in such a manner as to accent the good features and subdue the bad ones. Then too, minor faults can be turned into appealing beauty flaws that become more of an attraction than a detriment. Also, a face that has natural beauty but appears plain or lacking in accents, can be made to appear radiantly glamourous.

This reminds me of an occasion still fresh in my memory. Some years ago, my wife and I attended a school play that my son was in. After the play he introduced us to one of his teachers. During conversation with her, I noticed and became keenly intrigued by her plain and straightlaced appearance. Her hair was brushed straight back, tightly against her head. Her clothes, though neat, were plain and drab. Trying not to appear too obvious, I studied her face and noticed regular features, beautiful eyes, a clear complexion, and no make-up. Needless to say, the face presented a thoroughly "scrubbed look." The sight of this woman's face intrigued me because it offered a challenge!

17

5. The Well-Turned Leg

6. A Negligee

7. A Man's Shirt

8. The Eyes Have It

Tactfully, I persuaded her to come to my studio to be photographed. She arrived at the appointed time and I made an ordinary portrait of her, as she appeared, plain, drab and "mousy" looking.

As will be seen in Figure 9, the camera faithfully recorded her appearance without embellishment of any sort. Notice also, that although her features are symmetrical in their proportions, the face is obviously lacking in accents. After turning her over to my stylist for draping and make-up, I then carefully inspected her face and made some minor make-up corrections.

Figure 10 illustrates the end result. Immediately apparent are the accents produced by the use of make-up. The psychological glamour pattern suggests itself in the pantomime of the pose: the lowered eyelids, the emotional significance of her look, the submissive and sensuous quality of her full lips, and the forward thrust of her classic features. All these carefully arranged details enhance the natural feminine endowments with which nature has equipped her.

This leads us to conclude that a glamour portrait of a beautiful woman is not only produced by the pure mechanics of photography, but also because the photographer has added the expression and emotional significance of her femaleness.

The capacity to observe and to evaluate a woman with our eyes, our minds, and the camera confronts no greater challenge than esthetic and abstract nude photography. Our subject is the female form with it's multitude of variations in skeletal structure, in the modulations of flesh, and the play of light on the interrelated curves and masses of the body.

The attraction that a woman's nude figure holds for the eye of the photographer can be described on two emotional levels: In the first, he is like the placid cow in the pasture, calm, contented, and undisturbed by his surroundings. His work is unappealing and of poor quality. Or his interpretation is literal and savage, wherein appeal is directed to the earthy truth of raw reality—simply a woman without clothing (Figure 11).

The second level is much more complex: The photographer sees a woman's figure, not as it really is, but with an active mind and imagination. He pictures her as he would like her to be, in all the perfection of his lyrical and romantic mind. The physical attraction of her face or clothed body is no longer of great importance. Far greater is his idealizing conception of the harmonious contours of her nude form (Figure 12).

We have seen that glamour combines the realities of physical attraction and the intangibles of esthetics. Unifying these qualities in his work, the creative photographer portrays woman in such a manner that this fundamental quality is revealed. It is in this interpretation of suggestive femininity that the glamour photograph excels. The extent you can capture this quality on film depends upon the keenness of your perception, which boils down to

9. A Plain Appearance

10. The Glamour Pattern

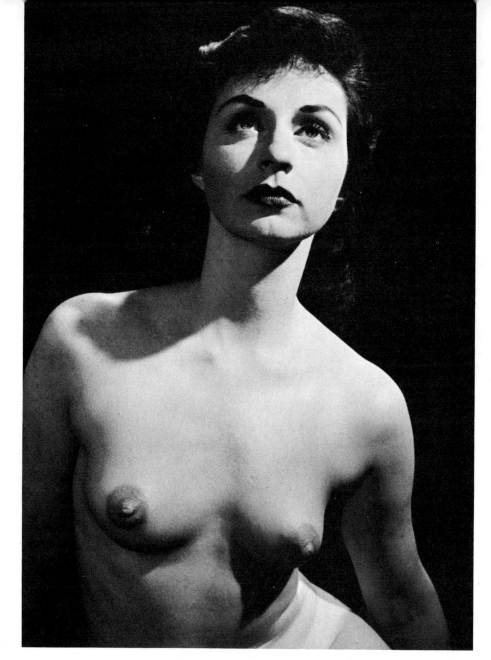

11. The Raw Impact of Reality

skill plus imagination. The methods you can employ will, of course, be largely governed by your model. With one model you may achieve an intense effect, whereas with another, you may have to deal more lightly.

Whether you approach glamour photography with the delicacy of a poet or with the proverbial ruggedness of the male; will depend upon your emotional capacities. That you must approach the making of a glamour photograph from the direction of physical attraction, is inevitable. A careful study of good glamour photography will reveal the truth of this statement.

22

Finally, you must never forget that the photographer of women does not deal with such commodities as sacks of potatoes or suits of clothes. His work is in the realm of art. Whatever exists in a beautiful woman as a result of her femininity, he brings into being, using his art as an intensifying medium. He captures the significance of an enticing look, or a winsome smile that beckons and says "Yes" to the beholder. He accents the charms of richly endowed curves and makes of them a thing of beauty. He portrays her with such magnetic force, that she becomes enchanting in her essential womanliness.

12. Idealizing the Nude Form

2
Faces and Figures

THE MAIN PURPOSE OF THIS CHAPTER IS TO ACQUAINT YOU WITH THE variety in the physical structure and coloring of the human female, the background of nature's evolutionary and environmental process and the role it plays in the structure of her face and figure. Without clothing it in scientific language, we will discuss this information as simply and as briefly as possible, so that those with no previous knowledge of the subject can understand the basic ideas. However, it will have been written in vain if we fail to realize that the understanding of the subject is essential to our work.

Also, we must not take a dogmatic attitude concerning the virtues of a particular type or breed of woman, or of any specific structural shape or size. As photographers, we should evaluate women's proportional differences as flexible factors which call for understanding and interpretation rather than qualities or inequalities to be condemned or praised because of our individual likes or dislikes. Nor can we argue the fact that no woman is endowed with flawless beauty. In a good glamour photograph, the impeccable perfection of a woman's face and figure is, at best a fleeting and fictitious illusion—one that has compelled the photographer to dig into his bag of tricks and come up with his technical "know how."

It appears then that there is more to an attractive woman than meets the eye at first glance. Instead of searching for an overall ideal, the creative worker makes the best of a woman's assets. He enhances her most attractive features, and in one way or another, subdues the imperfections. This is the basis for the photographer's success.

The incredible thing about a woman's physical charm is that her qual-

25

ities are not necessarily appealing to all men, but they are at times indefinable and beyond accurate description—quality that lies only in the eyes of the individual observer.

And then again, the elements of woman's qualities vary in relation to the period of time in which she lived. Through the ages, a beauty ideal is closely dependent upon the conquest of disease, knowledge of nutrition, health fads, and the fashions of the day.

If the paintings on their tombs are at all realistic, the ancient Egyptians and Mesopotamians were a willowy, slim people with narrow body proportions, long limbs, and sinewy muscles. The ideal Egyptian woman had an erect posture, square shoulders, flat stomach, and a high waistline.

The Minoan beauty around 1800 B.C. possessed a narrow waistline, round hips, and slender arms and legs. This ideal later gave way to the Greek form exemplified in the Aphrodite statues—tall, handsome, and fleshy figures but a far cry from the standards used in our contemporary American beauty contests.

The criteria of beauty for Medieval woman about 400 to 1400 A.D. was probably a product of bad living conditions. The thin emaciated look could only have been caused by improper diet and lack of exercise. According to medical authorities, the small under-developed breasts of that period seem to point to a combination of malnutrition and glandular malfunction. But with inherent feminine cleverness, the Medieval woman placed emphasis upon her role as the weaker sex, turning her physical inadequacies to her best advantage by changing them into beauty assets.

Centuries later, the Renaissance women 1400 to 1600 A.D. became the robust and curvatious figures of Rubens and Titian. Female anatomy of the times was typical of the bulges, creases, and profusion of body dimples recorded in the Rubens's nudes. This embellishment of the female flesh served as a yardstick for feminine beauty during this period.

The nineteenth century produced, through malnutrition and beauty diet, a slim languid version of a Greek hetaira (a type of Greek geisha girl), with a pale complexion, and in general, a sickly-looking maiden racked with tuberculosis.

Conversely, in the luxuriant late-Victorian and Edwardian periods, gluttonous eating produced a plump woman endowed with fleshy breasts and massive buttocks.

In the period following World War I, women sought to emulate the masculine figure by flattening their bustlines with tight bras, to emphasize the slim boyish body outline, and the flat shapelessness epitomized by the fashions of the "roaring twenties." Looking at that era in perspective, it is obvious that women looked neither boyish nor completely female, but something ridiculously in-between.

After World War II, the standard of physical beauty gradually changed to what nature had intended it to be, with the result that women of today look more feminine than they did at any time in their past history. With proper nutrition and exercise, their physiques have acquired a better bone formation, good muscle tone, clearer complexions, and healthier coloring. Their flesh contours are well apportioned and firmly formed. All in all, they are a healthier and better looking example of womanhood.

From an objective point of view, beauty is not limited by geographic boundaries, nor does it come in any specific size or shape. The crucial denominator is the body proportions and coloring that prevail in a particular country or racial group. Actually, women's faces and figures are differentiated by well-defined characteristics of heredity and environment. Ideal proportions and coloring vary in a multitude of subtle differences. Because different peoples set up their own standards, what is considered beauty in one ethnic group may not be in another. In the case of a distinct race or a subdivision thereof, beauty is usually determined by measuring it against a typical structure that has persisted in the strain and has thus become a standard of comparison.

Anthropologists tell us that a race is a biological group whose members possess certain physical traits in common. These traits are skin color: White, yellow, and black; head form: narrow, medium, and broad; and hair texture: straight, wiry, or curly and woolly. Other distinguishing characteristics are in the shape of the nose: thin, prominent, small, broad, flat; in the shape of the eyes: horizontal or oblique; in the color of the eyes: blue, gray, hazel, and brown; body structure: tall, short, narrow, or broad; the torso: long or short; the hips: narrow or broad; the breasts: concave, globular, pear-shaped, or pendulous; the legs: short or long.

This broad and general classification recognizes three primary races: Caucasian, Mongolian, and Negro. Since our discussion will be concerned with the Caucasian or white race, we will facilitate matters by excluding all others.

The white race is divided into three divisions: Mediterranean, Alpine, and Nordic.

The Mediterranean type (Figure 13) is best represented by the peoples of Southern Europe, around the Mediterranean Sea and parts of Western Europe. This racial type has a head that tends to be long and narrow. The complexion ranges from olive to white. The hair varies from dark brown to black and from straight to curly. The eyes range in color from medium to dark brown. The nose is likely to be straight and narrow and the lips well curved.

The Alpine type (Figure 14) is found in the region of the continent that includes White Russia, the Balkans, and Southern Germany. The pre-

13. The Mediterranean Face

14. The Alpine Face

dominent characteristics of this type differs from the Mediterranean in several respects. The head is generally broad with a high forehead and the face is also broader. The complexion is between dark and fair, the hair is predominantly brown but also may be blonde and straight to slightly wavy. Eye colors include blue, gray, hazel, and medium brown. The nose is small or large and is often broad, the mouth may be small and full-lipped or large with thin lips.

The Nordic type (Figure 15) appears to have developed in the Baltic regions of Eastern Scandinavia and Northern Germany. In its purest form, it is best represented by the natives of Norway and Sweden. The facial characteristics differ from the other two types in several respects, and therefore, constitute a third division. The Nordic head is oblong and high, the face long. The complexion is fair, being pink rather than white. The hair is mostly blonde and straight, but in some cases slightly curly. The eyes are blue or blue-gray. The nose is usually long and narrow with a prominent bridge. The mouth is generally full.

These three types are found in their purest forms on the European continent. But there is a fusion of one type with another. Consequently, there are types that are neither pure Mediterranean, nor Alpine, nor Nordic, but some-

28

15. The Nordic Face

16. The Irish Lassie

thing in-between. Moreover, these types are not necessarily confined to the regions specified. The Mediterranean type, for instance, is found in parts of Western Europe, Great Britain, along the West Coast of Scotland and Ireland, and in other parts of the world where the development of commerce and transportation has taken them.

There is an old saying, "the Viking conquerors came down from the north and the Spaniards came up from the south. Lo and behold! The beautiful Irish lassie with the beautiful blue eyes and the dark brown hair" (Figure 16).

Then too, a variety of physical traits can be witnessed in all parts of Europe. As examples, we would find that Spanish women are said to have the most beautiful eyes of any females in the world, but they are short in stature and in the legs. Most Italian women are short with wide hips and short legs, but they possess beautiful bustlines. French women seldom have beautiful legs, but they possess chic figures and narrow waistlines and their hips are very well proportioned. On the other hand, the English girl possesses the most beautifully proportioned legs on the European Continent. The South German girl has a wider hip structure than the North German. In comparison, the average Scandinavian girl is taller with a narrower body structure.

29

Other examples of the effects of human diversity can be seen in the densely populated industrial areas of the United States. The divisions of the white race in these areas have become modified examples of their European forebears. The results of intermarriage between Mediterraneans, Alpines, and Nordics can be seen in all parts of the United States. Because of this evolutionary medley, women's faces, figures, and coloring have become so diffuse that no sharp lines of heritage can now be drawn between them. What has emerged is a discernible American Type.

However, any description of the American type must, necessarily, be taken with a grain of salt if we are to apply it as a yardstick to the general female population of the United States. There are many physical traits and the subsequent operation of hereditary laws accounts for an infinite variety in physical structure and coloring. A description can do no more than illustrate the probability of being correct.

What is the American type? What is the ideal and what does she look like?

FACIAL SHAPES

Most American women have a more or less oval face which is the traditional ideal.

However, although the oval face is considered a standard of beauty, it does not necessarily follow that other facial contours are not beautiful, but merely that the oval face represents the ideal. We will also encounter facial contours that are triangular, heart, diamond, round, long, and square shaped.

Comparable in some respects to the oval shape, the triangular face is narrower at the temples than at the jaw line, and the cheeks are often full.

The heart-shaped face appears to be the opposite of the triangular face. Here the triangle is inverted, wide at the eyes and narrow at the jaw line, with a short and narrow pointed chin and full cheeks.

The diamond shaped face is broad at the cheek bones and tapers narrow at the temples and jaw line. The chin is often sharply pointed.

The round face is circular in shape, and there is a definite roundness to the contour and planes of the forehead, jaw line, and chin.

The long or oblong face is usually accompanied by a high forehead and a long chin. The jaw is slightly squared. Often the cheeks are hollow and the cheek bones prominent.

The square face has a wide jaw line and forehead. Sometimes, the chin and forehead are short, lending a marked square effect to the outline of the face.

30

If a face is divided into it's various sections, the division enables us to see that one quality that passes for beauty is a degree of regularity, a symmetrical coordination of the entire structure of the face. The eyes must not be so small that they appear "beady" or, for that matter, spaced too close together. Nor should the nose be so misshapen that it disturbs. The mouth, too, must not fall into unpleasant-looking lines with various facial expressions. In addition, there is the jaw, the chin, and the neck. All of these anatomical parts should coordinate into a pleasant symmetry.

The Eyes

The eyes are the most expressive element of the face. The various and ever-changing patterns of the facial muscles that activate them can produce a visual picture of all human emotions.

The important features of the eyes are their size, spacing, definition, slant of lids, and size of irises. It has been found that women with irises that are a little larger than normal are the most photogenic. Separation between the eyes should equal the width of either eye, measured in a straight line from corner to corner. And, of course, with modern make-up techniques, eyes can be made to appear larger, wider, and more defined (Figure 17).

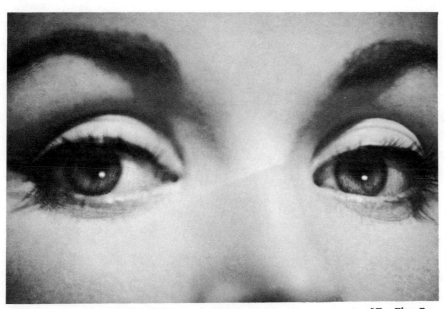

17. The Eyes   31

The Eyebrows

Insofar as facial beauty and expression are concerned, the eyebrows are an integral part of the eyes. The prettiest girls have natural-looking brows that are either wing shaped, arched with a slight degree of peak at their apex, or just slightly curved. Beginning at a point above the tear ducts, they are wider towards the nose and become thinner towards the ears. They also extend about ¼ to ½ inch beyond the outer corners of the eyes (Figure 18).

The Nose

The nose is the most important beauty feature of the face. In its ideal form it is not too long, too short, or too wide. In profile, it is straight or turned up a little at its end (Figure 19). In a full-faced view it is right in the middle of the face and does not tilt to one side or the other. The nose also has rounded planes with a delicate and clearly defined bone structure.

The Mouth

Today, the mouth of a beautiful woman is rarely without make-up. For many years now, the full, generous mouth has gained in popularity over the thin-lipped variety. Also, the sharply-pointed cupid's bows have given way to softly-rounded lines (Figure 20).

FIGURE PROPORTIONS

Statistics show that the average American girl has a short waist, large hips, small shoulders, and a longer, more shapely leg than her European forebears. She does not have large breasts, but they are not small either. Her body is well-rounded and curvy (Figure 21). The exception to this is the outdoor, athletic girl or the dancer. Her figure is sleek with tight smooth lines that lend themselves well to photographs illustrating action or dynamic interpretations (Figure 22).

While the physical characteristics of a model are dependent upon the specific needs of the intended photograph or the individual preferences of the photographer, current requirements for figure proportions and measurements fall into the following category:

Body proportions measured on the vertical plane of the figure (from head to toes without shoes) should be divided into four equal parts (Figure 23) as follows:

1. From the top of the head to the largest part of the bustline.

32

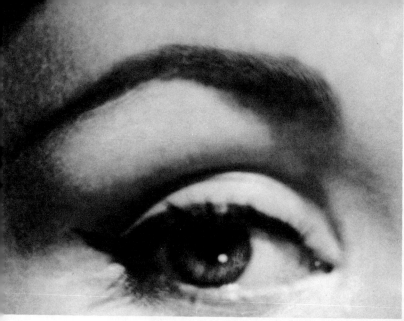

18. The Eyebrows

19. The Nose in Profile

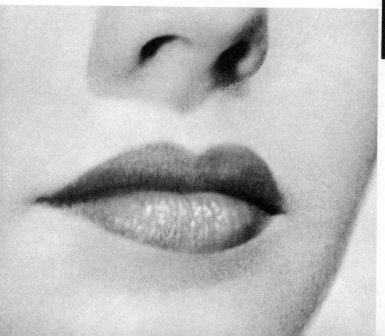

20. The Mouth

22. The Slim Figure

23. Body Proportions

2. From the bustline to the top of the hip bone.
3. From the hip to the center of the knee bone.
4. From the knee to the floor.

Body proportions measured on the horizontal planes of the figure: Give or take one or two inches, hips and bust that measure 36 inches at their largest parts should have a waistline 10 inches less or 26 inches in all. These dimensions may be scaled up or down. However, proportions should be about the same, with measurements changing with the model's height. As an example: hips and bust that measure 34 inches should have a waist measuring 24 inches. For photographic purposes, the model's height is relatively unimportant if her proportions, on a vertical plane, divide into four equal parts as illustrated in Figure 23.

To summarize: We have established that the many racial stocks, intermingling of the three divisions of the white race, and the subsequent variation in body structure make it difficult and impractical to set an exact standard of beauty. We can even conclude that so-called beauty experts cannot possibly define the measurements of "the perfect female" in any final word.

From what we have learned, we can readily understand that, as photographers of women, we may expect to find intriguing problems of faces and figures presenting themselves before our cameras. If our work is to be of a high standard, we will, at times, have to resort to the use of corrective procedures. Elsewhere in this book we will discuss these measures.

3
Costume Elements

APART FROM THE PHOTOGRAPHER'S IMAGINATION AND SKILL, WHAT CAN STIR a man's imagination more effectively than the charm of a beautiful woman's curvy figure dressed in costume elements that reveal and conceal to a point where she appears provocative and alluring? A Bikini bathing suit, a filmy night gown, a low-cut evening gown, a leotard, falsies—these are ingredients to improve on nature's handiwork and increase physical attraction.

Clearly we need to understand the psychological aspects of selecting various costume elements. Carefully employed, they will enhance the model's physical charm and help to impart to a photograph that magnetic force called "glamour."

But first, let us borrow for our use one of the laws of costume design generally accepted by women's fashion experts—the design considerations of "The Seductive Impulse" theory. In practice, this theory takes into account woman's secondary sex characteristics: the bust, the waist or abdomen, the hips, the buttocks, and the legs. Attention can be focused on one or more of these areas by accenting them with fabric stretched tightly over them, or by padding the areas to make them appear larger.

We can readily understand that these design techniques of concealment and implied revelation are primarily methods resorting to an elusive addition or subtraction of body lines and proportions. This is one method of creating a visual impact upon the male viewer.

It must now be evident that a well-rounded girl squeezed into a scanty bathing suit or dressed in a filmy negligee can often appear more provocative and radiate more appeal than if she were in the nude. Simply stated, that

39

24. Breast Cleavage

"magic something" can be enhanced by the art of concealing and revealing of natural attributes with the aid of costume elements. Remembering this, let us examine some examples of the basic strategy of modern dress and undress and the subsequent effect of these devices on the model:

In Figure 24, attention is directed to a particular body area—the bustline and its breast cleavage. The neckline of the garment reveals and conceals this famous area of the well-developed model. A low-cut evening gown or a revealing negligee can also be used to produce a similar effect.

In Figure 25, the viewed impact is that of the over-all structure of the body. Visual attention is created by the use of a body-clinging leotard that calls attention to the flowing lines and contours of the model's chic figure. The high cut at the sides of the garment produces the illusion of longer leg lines. A Bikini or a high-cut panty brief and french bra also serve the same purpose.

In Figure 26, the sleek fit of the mesh stockings accents the beauty of the model's well turned legs. Mesh stockings may also be worn with other costume elements. They combine ideally with skin tight leotards, dance rehearsal, and theatrical costumes in general.

25. Body Clinging Leotard

26. Mesh Stockings

DRAPING FOR HEAD AND SHOULDER PORTRAITS

Here you will find techniques of draping from which you can simulate, in head and shoulder portraits, many effective and flattering evening gown styles.

Draping Material

At your nearest yard goods or department store select a few pieces of light or dark color materials such as tulle, marquisette, chiffon velvet, faille crepe or any other soft material that may catch your fancy. Select pieces ¾ yard wide by 2 yards long; also pieces ½ yard by 2 yards long. All these materials will drape gracefully.

42

Anchoring Belts

Because of inadequate methods of anchoring, most old-fashioned draping techniques are awkward and cumbersome for the photographer as well as for the model. To replace the old method, we shall use a simple elastic belt with a hook and eye arrangement to anchor the draping material at the waistline and thus make for quick and efficient adjustments at the shoulders and neckline. In other words, while gathering or pulling the material taut at the shoulders and neckline, the elastic belt serves as an anchorage for the material at the waist.

Get a 2 inch wide elastic belting, 30 inches long. Sew a hook at one end, and then start at the other end of the belt and sew 6 eyes, 2 inches apart. The eyes will accommodate different waistline sizes.

With some draping styles, a second belt will be required. Buy ½ or ¾ inch wide elastic belting 30 inches long. Sew a buckle at one end for fastening at desired lengths. This belt is to be used for those draping styles that require the material to be pulled down and anchored at the back of the drape.

Strapless Half-Brassiere

Brassieres with shoulder straps cannot successfully be hidden from view in a draping style that fully exposes the shoulders. We must, therefore, have on hand strapless bras which produce an uplift and which cover only the lower part of the bust as shown in Figure 27. Naturally, you will find it necessary to have on hand various size bras. Avail yourself of three sizes: "A" (small), "B" (medium), and "C" (large).

27. Strapless Brassiere

Off-the-Shoulder Drape

Double a piece of ¾ yard wide material and draw it high around the back of the model's shoulders and cross it over the bust as shown in Figure 28. Now ask your model to hold the material securely in place while you fasten the anchoring belt tightly over the material at the waistline. Anchoring the belt at this point will now enable you to adjust the drape into soft folds at the shoulder line.

Strapless Evening Gown

The draping arrangement shown in Figure 28 can readily be changed into a strapless evening gown style by drawing the material underneath the armpits rather than over the arms. The finished draping style is shown in Figure 29.

28. Off-the-Shoulder Drape

29. Strapless Evening Gown

30. Plunging Halter Neckline

Plunging Halter Neckline

Double a piece of ½ yard material and draw it around the back of t.
model's neck. Then bring it straight down over the bust. Do not, however,
cross the material. At this point, ask the model to hold the drape securely
in place while you fasten the anchor belt tightly at the waist. Look at the
plunging halter neckline in Figure 30.

Strapped Evening Gown

Double a piece of ½ yard wide material and draw it loosely around the
back of the model's neck. Then cross it over the bust and ask the model to
hold the drape in place while you fasten the anchor belt over the material
at the waist. You are now ready to use the buckle belt I mentioned previ-

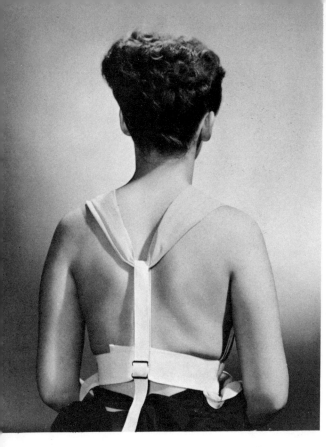

31. The Buckle Belt

32. Strapped Evening Gown

ously. Loop the buckle belt through the material at the back of the neck and also under the anchor belt at the waist. Now draw the buckle belt tight and buckle it as shown in Figure 31. You may now fasten a small attractive clip on each side of the front of the drape. The finished drape should appear as shown in Figure 32.

Bare-Back Evening Gown

To stress the importance of the buckle belt, you will find it invaluable in draping for profile, three-quarter view, and over-the-shoulder poses wherein the model's back is to be complimented.

A beautifully exposed back effect can be achieved by placing a piece of ¾ yard wide material on the model's shoulders. Now carry it down over the bust and fasten the material with the anchor belt at the waist. Then loop the buckle belt through the material at the back of the neck and also through the anchor belt at the waist. Draw the buckle belt tight and fasten it. Also adjust the drape as shown in Figure 33.

33. Bare-Back Evening Gown

4
Make-up and Its Application

PERFECT FACIAL BEAUTY AND SYMMETRY HAVE BEEN BESTOWED UPON VERY few women. Despite this, less fortunate women can still be made attractive. This is accomplished with the subtle use of make-up, applied in such a manner as to accent the good features and subdue the bad ones. Moreover, in many cases, minor facial faults can be turned into appealing beauty flaws, that become more attractive than detrimental. Thus, faces which are fairly attractive can very well take on the illusion of exciting beauty.

Because you may be called upon to produce good work with faces that present imperfections in their parts, you should become skilled in the proper use of make-up. With this knowledge you can subdue the imperfections and impart beauty to the face.

At first thought, you may reason that the art of make-up is intricate and entails a great deal of time and effort. Your impression may also be that corrections can be accomplished with retouching. Both suppositions are wrong. To begin with, there are some corrections easily made with make-up that are almost impossible to correct with retouching. This is especially true with the small size films, which are used in the popular 35mm and 2¼ x 2¼ reflex cameras. Furthermore, there are very few retouchers capable of making corrections as efficiently as those which are possible with a few simple tricks of make-up. The word "simple" is used in its literal sense, for once you have learned some of the techniques and have become proficient in their use, you will be able to apply them quickly and easily.

The subject of retouching is a complicated one and the acquisition of this skill is not easy. Since the subject could not be covered adequately in this book, the reader is directed to books specializing in photographic retouching.

Whether or not to use make-up will depend upon your judgment and the facial characteristics of your models. There will be instances when you have both the time and the opportunity to apply a complete make-up. At such times you can bring all your skill into play. Then again you may find that only a corrective application is necessary.

In this and the following chapter we will discuss two general make-up techniques:

1. Make-up and its application: Techniques employed in the complete make-up of a face.
2. Corrective Make-up: Techniques for corrections to parts of the face where it is necessary to alter specific defects.

There are many make-up products currently on the market which will serve our purpose adequately. Almost any well known name-brand will do. However, it is a good policy to keep abreast of the latest developments in make-up. Old types are constantly being improved upon and new ones are being developed by Hollywood's top make-up artists as well as the make-up manufacturers who supply them. The new materials eventually become available to the professional still photographer and to the amateur hobbyist.

Because a great deal can be accomplished with relatively few make-up materials, we can keep the number required to the barest minimum. As you acquire proficiency and greater need, you may add other materials.

The following is a tentative list of make-up materials which you should acquire at the start:

Foundation (two shades)
Face powder (matching shades for the foundations)
Cheek rouge (cake or paste) to be used only for color phootgraphy.
Eye shadow (brown and blue-gray)
Lip sticks (deep red, light red, and orange-red)
Eyebrow pencils (black, dark brown, and light brown)
Mascara (black and dark brown)
Powder puffs
Sponge (for pancake application)
Brushes (lip brush, eyebrow brush, eyelash brush, and powder brush)
Miscellaneous (white vaseline, cleansing cream, astringent lotion, facial tissue, and towels)

In addition, if you intend to do corrective make-up, you will require a foundation three shades lighter than normal and a foundation three shades darker than normal.

FOUNDATION

The base or make-up foundation, as it is usually referred to by make-up artists and beauty consultants, is the first and most important step in the creation of a good make-up. When used correctly, it covers and disguises complexion flaws such as blotches, discolorations, freckles, large pores, and other blemishes. A good foundation will also hide fatigue lines, lighten or darken the skin, add color to a sallow complexion, and in general, produce a satin-smooth skin tone.

There are three types of foundation: Liquid, cream base (packaged in a stick, a tube, or jar), and pancake, which comes in a dry form. These are commonly available for street make-up. In addition, there is the professional grease paint which is used for stage, television, and screen. As far as covering power is concerned, there is no substitute for the professional brands of cream, grease paint, and pancake. The cream and the professional grease paint require a matching powder.

That the foundation should match the model's natural skin tone is a point that needs clarification. There are many variations in skin tones, and this factor alone would require the acquisition of many foundation shades. For practical purposes, however, what is actually needed is two average shades, one for the olive tone complexion and another for the fair complexion. They can also be interchanged. For example, if a brunette happens to have a somewhat fair skin, use the fair complexion foundation. On the other hand, if a blonde or a redhead has an olive tone skin, use an olive tone foundation.

In the professional brands prepared for stage and screen, make-up manufacturers designate specific foundation shades by numbers. Thus, if a basic shade is designated as No. *25*, three shades lighter is usually marked No. *22*, while three shades darker is marked No. *28*. Bear in mind that each manufacturer has his own names and numbers for specific make-up colors and shades.

Whether you use a cream base or pancake foundation for your model's face, you will find pancake easier to apply and more effective for the neck, shoulders, arms, and other exposed body areas. This is especially true for beach photography where sand tends to adhere to a cream base foundation.

CHEEK ROUGE

Cheek rouge should never be used in black and white photography, because it creates a receding effect to the area it is applied to. However, it should be used in color photography where it adds color contrast and radiance to the complexion.

50

Cheek rouge comes in a cream or in a dry cake form. The cream is the easiest to apply because it blends better and produces a more natural effect. The dry rouge can be used for touch-up after the make-up is completed.

Use a light color rouge for a fair complexion and a darker color for the olive tone complexion.

EYE SHADOW

Eye shadow is used as a method of eye framing, wherein the beauty of the eyes are accented and set-off to advantage. Eye shadow also adds contour and makes the eyes look larger.

FACE POWDER

With a cream base foundation, a matching shade of face powder is used to produce a normal sheen to the skin. The face should not appear greasy from too much foundation or not enough powder. Nor should the face appear dull from the excessive use of powder. A powder is not required with a pancake foundation.

EYEBROWS

The eyebrows give expression and framing to the eyes. Although the natural line of the brows can be changed in shape or length, as a rule, they should follow the contour of the upper curve of the eyes. They should also extend about ¼ to ½ inch out and beyond the outer corners of the eyes.

Use a black eyebrow pencil for dark brown or black hair, a dark brown pencil for medium brown hair, and a light brown pencil for blonde and red hair.

MASCARA

Because the eyes are the most expressive feature of a beautiful woman, proper make-up should be used to enhance their expressiveness as well as their beauty. This helps to create a more glamourous effect.

Mascara is a preparation for darkening the eyelashes, thus creating greater contrast and subtle framing of the eyes. The best mascara comes prepared in a waterproof cream or cake form and it is applied directly to the eyelashes. Use black mascara for black or dark brown hair, a dark brown mascara for blonde, red, and medium brown hair.

LIPSTICK

Lipstick is used to create proper contour and contrast against the other features of the face. In general, the lipstick should follow the natural lip lines. There are, however, lips that require alterations. Some need to be made larger while others need to be made smaller or changed in their outline. This will be discussed more fully in the next chapter.

For color photography, use a deep red lipstick for a brunette with an olive tone complexion. Use a light red lipstick for a blonde with a fair complexion. Use an orange-red lipstick for a redhead with fair complexion. In black and white photography the monochromatic values will be essentially correct and perfectly suited for use with modern panchromatic films.

PRELIMINARY PREPARATION

Because the application of make-up entails the risk of soiling your model's clothing with foundation or powder, be kind to her and provide a protective towel, or make-up bib.

Instruct her to remove her regular street make-up by applying cleansing cream and wiping it off completely with face tissues. Following this, you can apply an astringent lotion to the face, such as witch hazel. The astringent serves two purposes, to remove the last particles of cleansing cream and to close the facial pores.

APPLYING THE FOUNDATION

Figure 34 illustrates a face without make-up. Although the model's features are more or less symmetrical, the absence of make-up results in a lack of accents. We might say that the face is devoid of sparkle or that quality we call glamour.

The quality of the finished make-up depends largely upon the amount and the manner in which the foundation is applied. If too much is used, the final result will appear mask-like and unnatural. To insure a good make-up, the foundation should be used sparingly. Furthermore, if a minimum amount is applied, we need not necessarily use powder over the foundation. Thus we can reproduce a velvety and highlighted skin texture.

Although other methods of applying a cream foundation have been advocated, the following method is very efficient, since it lends control to the procedure: With the tip of your finger, apply the foundation sparingly in a stipple or dots over the entire face (Figure 35).

52

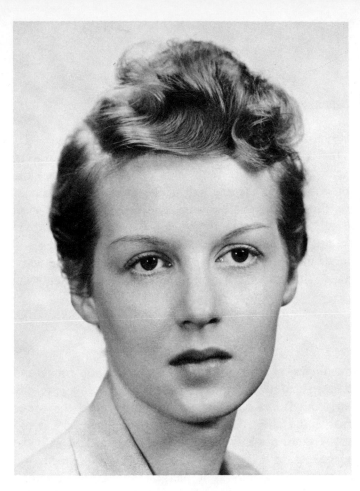

34. The Face Without Make-up

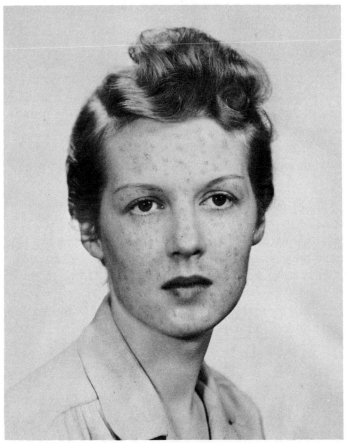

35. Applying the Foundation Cream

SPREADING THE FOUNDATION

Place your fingers against the skin and gently pat and pull into all the surrounding areas of the dots (Figure 36). The foundation must not be rubbed in, but gently patted and pulled evenly over the surface of the skin. As you come close to the hair-line, pat and pull in the direction of the hair, carrying the foundation precisely to the hair-line, and not just a little short of it. Blend the cream out and onto the ears (if they are to be exposed), over the jaw, and onto the neck. Blending the foundation in this manner will insure against a definite demarcation of color between the face and the neck. Finally, inspect the face, smoothing here and there until the foundation finally appears even.

CHEEK ROUGE

With the tip of your finger, pick up a small amount of cream rouge and sparingly pat three or four separate dots on the cheek bones. Now carefully and delicately blend the rouge dots with the foundation. Spread the rouge a little beyond the area of the cheek bones. However, do not carry it too close to the hairline at the sides, nor any lower than a point in line with the end of the nose. Also, make sure that the deepest shade of color begins on the cheek bones and gradually lightens as it merges into the surrounding areas.

EYE SHADOW

With your finger, pick up a small amount of eye shadow and place it along the upper lids, close to the eyelash line (Figure 37). Now gradually spread the shadow upward and outward, fading the shadow into the foundation as you reach the eyebrows and the outer corners of the eyes. Eye shadow should be applied heaviest on the eyelids. Do not use shadow on the inner corners of the eyes, unless your subject has a flat or wide nose bridge.

FACE POWDER

Now inspect the make-up carefully from all angles. In the event that you find imperfections, repair them at this point in the make-up. For, once you apply powder, it is not easy to make corrections, particularly to the foundation base.

Charge a powder puff with the matching powder and apply it with a patting motion over the entire face, on the ears (if they are exposed), under the

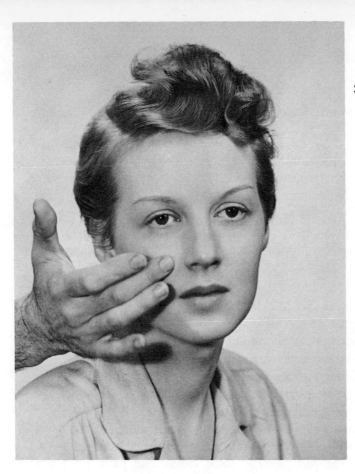

36. Spreading the Foundation Cream

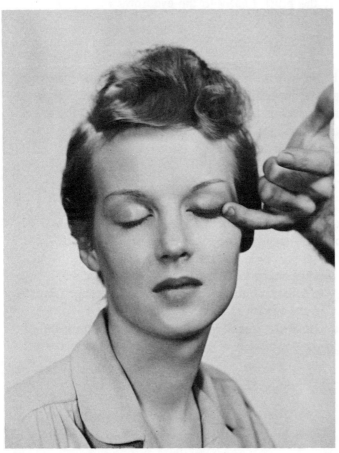

37. Eye Shadow

jaw, and on the neck. Do not, under any circumstances, rub the powder into the foundation.

Allow the powder to set for a minute or two and then remove any excess powder with the powder brush.

EYE BROWS

Sharpen the eyebrow pencil to a wedge-sharped edge, then fill in any area in the eyebrows that may show as slight patches of skin. Apply the pencil in short strokes to simulate the hair of the eyebrows and their normal direction.

The line of the eyebrows should extend about ½ inch beyond the outer corners of the eyes (Figure 38). This extension you will have to judge for yourself. Moreover, discretion at this point is in order because there are no two faces that can take the same treatment.

In the extension of the eyebrows, again apply the eyebrow pencil in short strokes, simulating the natural direction of the hair of the eyebrows rather than creating a continuous straight line.

For eyebrows that are well shaped but require darkening, define them in this manner: place white vaseline in the palm of your hand, rub the eyebrow pencil into it and pick up the color from your palm onto the eyebrow brush; then apply the brush lightly to the eyebrows.

MASCARA

Moisten the eyelash brush with water, shake out the excess, and rub over the cake of mascara. Start at the center areas of the eyes (Figure 39) and brush the lashes of the upper eyelids from roots to tips, working to the outer edges of the eyes. Apply the mascara heaviest at the outer edges. Now very lightly mascara the lashes of the lower lids.

LIP STICK

Most women, through constant practice, have acquired the knack of making up their own lips. You should encourage them to do so, with these additional instructions:

1. Draw the line of the lips sharp and clearly defined (Figure 40).
2. Carry the lip rouge to fullest mouth width, extending the rouge inward and to the corners of the mouth.
3. After rouging the upper lip, press lips together; the impression of the upper lip upon the lower one will register approximately correct on the lower lip.

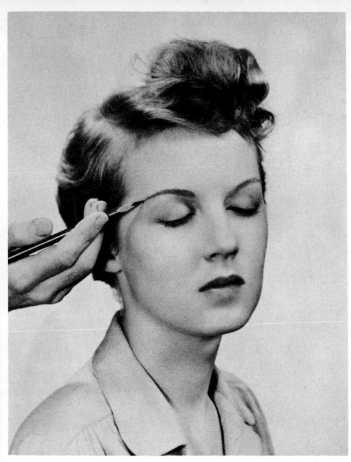

38. The Eyebrows

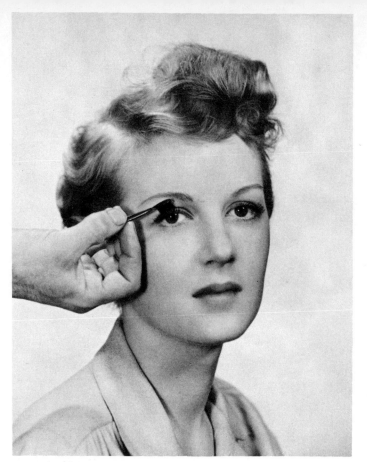

39. Mascara

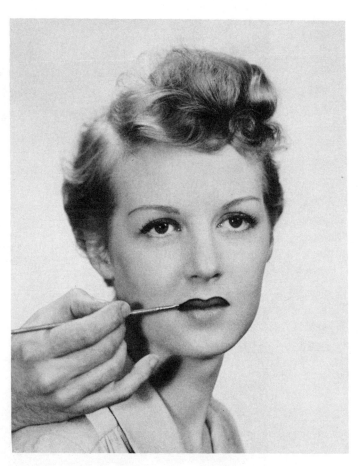

40. The Lips

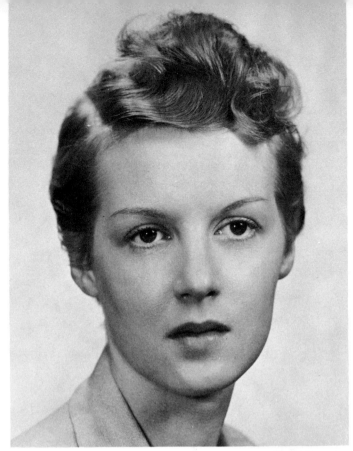

41. Before Make-up

42. After Make-up

4. Make sure the lower lip is the same width as the upper lip.

5. Draw the line of the lower lip so that it is sharply defined.

6. Blot excess lip rouge with face tissue.

FINISHING TOUCHES

Again carefully inspect the make-up for imperfections. Go over the eyebrows with an eyelash brush. Lightly pat a small touch of white vaseline on the lips to give them a pleasant highlight. Figures 41 and 42 illustrate before and after make-up.

5
Corrective Make-up

AT THE OUTSET, A DISTINCTION SHOULD BE MADE AND KEPT IN MIND. THERE is a difference between a simple make-up and a corrective one. It is a difference not only in purpose but also in technique.

The last chapter dealt primarily with the application of simple make-up. As we have learned, simple make-up is designed to minimize or eliminate skin blemishes, produce smooth skin textures and lend accents here and there. Corrective make-up, on the other hand, deals selectively with the modification of facial contours.

The principles of corrective make-up are in accord with the production of a monochromatic image. Tonal values of the various parts of the face can be subdued into a lower hue or accented into a higher value. Actually, areas that are darkened in tone with the use of make-up will appear to recede or look smaller, while those areas that are made lighter will appear to stand out or look larger. Employing this principle, a crooked nose can be made to appear straight, a long nose to appear shorter, small eyes to appear larger, and a fat face, thinner.

After you have become adept in the use of corrective make-up, it may be a triumph of technique on your part to be able to change facial contours to conform with your own judgment and artistic perception. Nevertheless, even though your models may feel flattered momentarily with the new facial modeling, they will be just as quick to notice in their finished photographs the inevitable change in likeness. Needless to say, "they will not like it." The point to be made is that corrections of facial contours is a proper undertaking, provided the corrections do not change the likeness of the face. And then too, only prominent facial faults should be corrected. Common sense, therefore, dictates that restraint should, at all times, be used.

Corrections of facial contours should follow the application of the foundation color. This procedure was described in the last chapter.

NARROWING A BROAD NOSE

If the nose is broad and you wish to narrow it, very lightly apply a three shade darker-than-normal foundation on both sides of the nose, within the areas shown in Figure 43.* Very delicately, blend the color evenly as you reach the outer edges of the working area, fading it gradually into the surrounding foundation. Otherwise, there may be a definite demarcation of color. Upon close inspection the color should appear merged with the surrounding area of foundation.

WIDENING A THIN NOSE

To widen a thin nose, follow the procedure as outlined above, with this exception: in the areas under discussion use a three shade lighter-than-normal foundation.

CORRECTING A FLAT NOSE

If the nose is flat, you can correct this fault by making the bridge of the nose appear higher. To do this, apply the lighter foundation down the center of the nose (Figure 44). Then, gradually blend the color into the surrounding areas on the bridge of the nose.

* The shadows and highlights of the facial areas in this series of illustrations have been sharply defined. This will enable you to more easily follow the instructions contained in this chapter.

43. Narrowing a Broad Nose

44. Correcting a Flat Nose

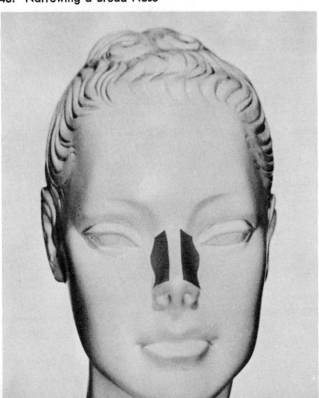

SHORTENING A LONG NOSE

If the nose is long and you wish to make it appear shorter, apply the darker foundation on the under side of the nose (Figure 45). Then, gradually blend the color onto the tip of the nose.

NARROWING A WIDE JAW

Narrowing a wide jaw is accomplished by applying the darker foundation on the jaw line (Figure 46). Then, gradually blend the color lighter and lighter into the surrounding areas of foundation.

LENGTHENING A SHORT CHIN

A short chin may be made to appear longer by applying the lighter foundation on the lower edge of the chin as outlined above. Then, gradually fade the color off into the surrounding areas.

SHORTENING A LONG CHIN

To shorten a long chin apply the darker foundation on the lower edge of the chin (Figure 47). Then, gradually fade the color off into the surrounding areas of foundation.

THINNING A HEAVY OR ROUND FACE

A face that is too heavy or too round may be made to appear narrower or thinner by applying the darker foundation just below the cheek bones as shown in (Figure 48). Then, gradually blend the color delicately and fade it into the surrounding areas of foundation.

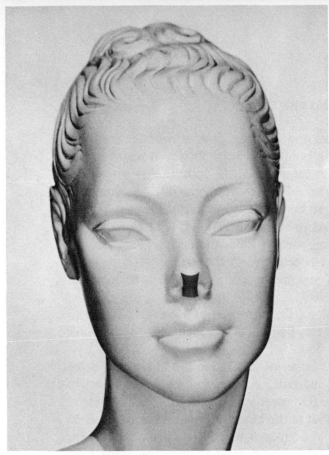

45. Shortening a Long Nose

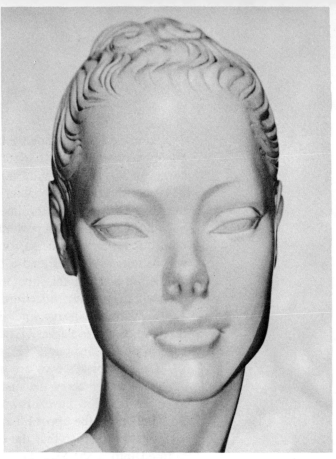

46. Narrowing a Wide Jaw

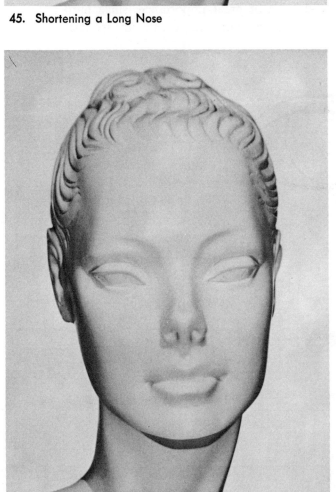

47. Shortening a Long Chin

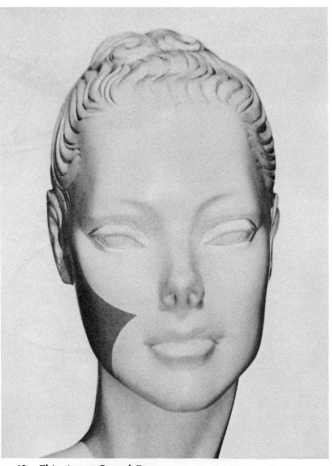

48. Thinning a Round Face

To make the eyes appear larger and brighter, draw a light line with the black eyebrow pencil (the starting point is about half-way from the inner corner of the lower eyelid, close to the roots of the lashes) and extend the line ⅛ inch beyond the outer corner of the eye (Figure 49). As you near the outer corner, draw the line straight. In the extension of the line beyond the outer corner, it is important that you taper the line off lighter and lighter until it fades in with the surrounding area of foundation. Otherwise, the line will be noticeable and lend a hard appearance to the eyes.

Before starting this operation you might ask your subject to look up. This will make your procedure easier.

Next, draw a heavy line all along the upper lid as close as possible to the base of the eyelashes. Extend this line about ¼ inch beyond the outer edge in an upward curve (Figure 50).

If your subject's eyes are quite large, do not curve the line at the outer edge, but rather carry the line to the outer corner of the eye and down to meet the line you have drawn on the lower eyelid, at the area they meet. Both the line of the upper lid and that of the lower lid should now be softened with the finger tip so that the end of both lines blend and become somewhat diffused into a shadow. This procedure is of great importance, since hard lines would show in the finished photograph and thus create an artificial effect.

49. Lining the Lower Eyelid

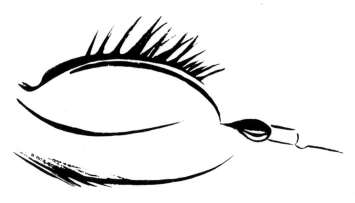

50. Lining the Upper Eyelid

Prominent or Protruding Eyes

Apply the eye shadow as outlined in the last chapter, but use a darker than normal shade.

Deep-Set Eyes

Apply the eye shadow as outlined in the last chapter, but use a lighter than normal shade, or, do not use eye shadow at all.

Close-Set Eyes

To create the illusion of greater width, start the eye shadow a little distance from the inner corners of the eyes and blend the shadow to a deeper shade towards the outer corners of the eyes.

THE LIPS

In your work you may encounter malformations of the mouth that affect the contour of the lips. Some may be caused by defective dental structure and bad alignment of the teeth. Other malformations are caused by defective jaw structure.

Without going into a detailed discussion of these defects, it will suffice to say that they should be rectified or at least minimized by proper make-up correction. Otherwise, the defects will be apparent in a photograph.

Although most women know how to apply lip rouge, needless to say, you should learn to make corrections of the contours and lines of the lips yourself.

The application of lip rouge as a corrective, although seemingly simple, is however, one of the most difficult techniques in make-up application. Since the work primarily entails the drawing of clean, sharp, curving outlines, you should do plenty of practicing if you intend to become proficient in lip corrections.

The Practice Step

With the lip brush, draw in the outline of the upper lip. Starting at the center of the lip, draw to the outer corners. The lower lip line is then drawn and the lips filled in.

51. Upper Lip with a Shallow Bow

Cupid's Bow and Arch

Figure 51 illustrates an upper lip with a shallow bow. The lip appears straight and stern.

To correct this fault, start in the center of the lip, follow the natural line for about ⅛ inch, then carry the color above the natural line and curve the bow upward and outward, as shown by the dotted line. On the downstroke, curve or arch the sides slightly as you work towards the corners of the mouth. This will lend a pleasant expression to the lips.

52. Upper Lip with a Sharply Pointed Bow

Sharply Pointed Bow

Figure 52 illustrates a sharply pointed bow that gives the lips a pinched appearance. The procedure in this case is quite simple: Fill in the areas as designated by the dotted line, being careful to keep a slight bow.

Thin Upper Lip

The correction of a thin upper lip requires the application of lip rouge above the confines of the natural lip lines.

Start in the center of lip and work out to the corners, being careful to follow the natural contour of the lip. The dotted line in Figure 53 illustrates this point.

53. A Thin Upper Lip

Thin Lower Lip

The correction of a thin lower lip also requires the application of lip rouge beyond the confines of the natural lip line.

Extend the line of the lower lip as illustrated by the dotted line in Figure 54. Be careful, however, that both upper and lower lip are equal in size.

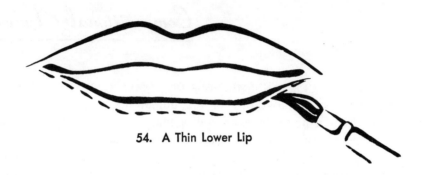

54. A Thin Lower Lip

Unsymmetrical Upper Lip

A fault you will often find is an unsymmetrical upper lip. Carefully build up the narrower side to match the wider one.

Wide Mouth

A mouth that is wide can be made to appear narrower by stopping the rouge line just short of the corners of the lips.

Narrow Mouth

A mouth that is narrow can be made to appear wider by extending the rouge line beyond the corners of the lips.

67

6
Compositional Elements

THE ESTABLISHED RULES AND METHODS OF COMPOSITION IN ART DO NOT always apply to the photography of the human form, primarily, because depicting the human figure is essentially a matter of arranging its elements in a plastic and plausible manner. Compositional treatment of a still-life, a seascape, or a landscape is limited by the immovable nature of the subject, but with the human form, we must arrange the line and mass pattern of the figure to form a pantomime of motion, intended motion, or restful inactivity.

However, to assume that there are no definite rules for composition in photography is a fallacy that we will dispense with immediately. Although the rules cannot be arbitrarily laid down like a law, nevertheless, each photographic situation requires its own individual arrangement, including an understanding of some of the elementary principles of composition.

DOMINANT POINT OF INTEREST

In its broadest sense, effective composition is the arrangement of each element in the picture in relation to its importance to the whole theme. Each separate element contributes to a greater or lesser degree, by emphasis or subordination. We make use of an age-old principle: "the dominant point of interest."

For example, in Figure 55 our eyes are immediately drawn to the largest black crystal in the design. Our gaze does not wander at any point; rather, it is directed straight towards the crystal.

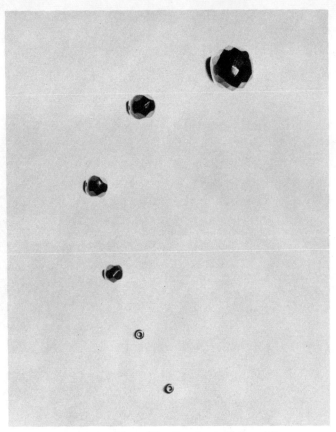

55. Dominant Point of Interest

In Figure 56 the principle is shown in actual application. The eye is attracted to the most dominant area within the illustration and progresses within the picture area in the same manner as with the crystals. Also, the effect of contrast serves to.capture and fix the attention on the most desirable area. We may, therefore, assume that the focal point of interest can be emphasized and attracted to the eye by size, by contrast, by brightness, as in Figure 57; or at the other extreme, by being made the least illuminated area of the whole composition, as in Figure 58. The entire principle depends largely on your treatment of the dominant point of interest. It is of paramount importance that you impress this fact on your memory, because it is the basis of all good composition.

In Figure 59, we discover another method of confining attention to the main theme: by lighting a controlled area in back of the figure and darkening the area towards the edges of the picture frame. The figure is set off, away from the background, guiding the eye immediately and naturally to the dominant point of interest.

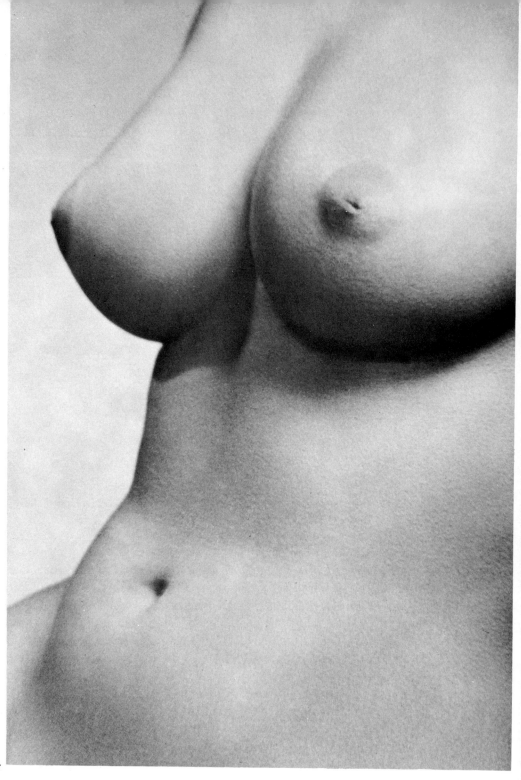

56. Dominant Point of Interest

57. Accents with Light Areas

58. Accents with Dark Areas

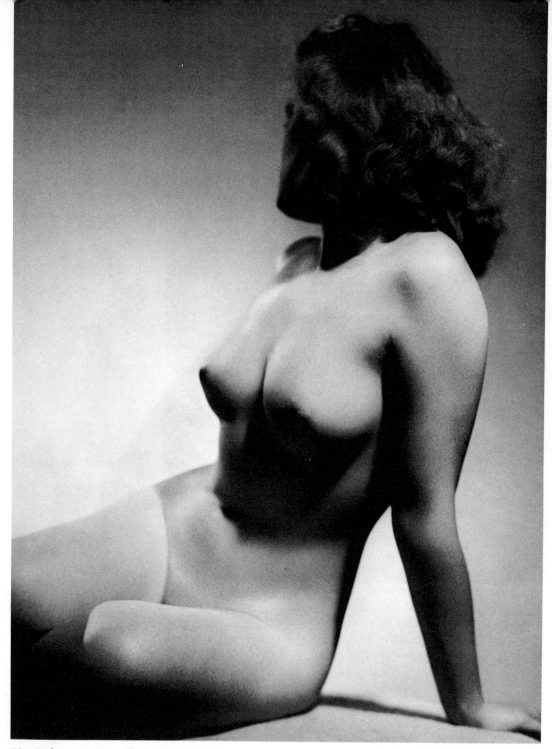

59. Lighting a Controlled Area on Background

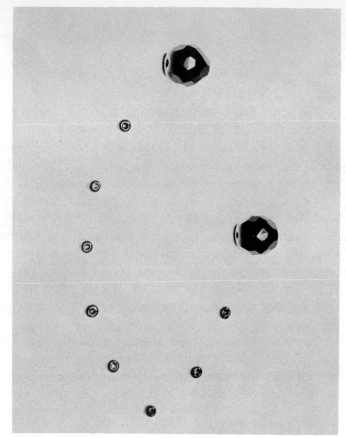

60. Divided Interest

In Figure 60, attention is divided between the large black crystals, forcing the eyes to divide their interest between two different areas. Unable to focus on both crystals at the same time, our eyes leap back and forth, for they cannot fix themselves upon one dominant point. We can therefore assume that secondary points of interest must be made less dominant, either in size or tone; otherwise, it can lead to confusion.

The dominant point of interest will be supported by details of secondary importance, which will be placed as close to the primary point as the subject will permit, so the eyes may readily grasp the relationship. Secondary points of interest will be placed in secondary positions, in the proper scale of tones. Other supporting points will take their relative positions in the picture area and in the tonal scale.

We often find ourselves turning to nature for guidance in composition, for there is a kind of "frame" around everything we see in the world. Unless we turn or bend, we do not see what is above our heads or at our feet, but within the frame of our vision, we do see a horizon where sky and earth or sea appear to converge, approximately at eye level.

Through centuries, we have become accustomed to seeing things at this level. We revert to this natural principle of vision when we locate the dominant point of interest. In a picture area, this should be located somewhere along the upper half of a diagonal line drawn from a lower corner to its opposite corner in the upper part of the picture, as in Figures 61 and 62. There are, of course, any number of exceptions to this rule: some sitting, kneeling, stooping, or reclining body attitudes require more space above the figure.

There is a broad field in the use of space division. The camera being what it is, an instrument that records everything placed in front of it, does not in itself omit distracting or uninteresting elements in a composition. This is the function of the phototgrapher. His skill can be measured by his aptitude

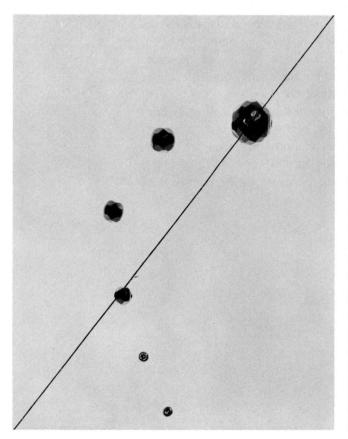

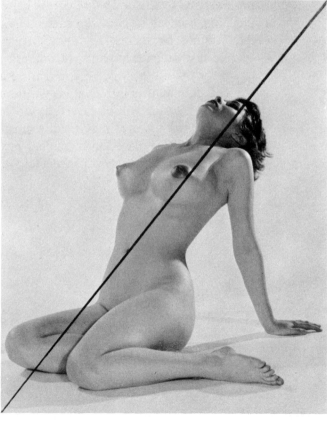

61. Space Division

62. Space Division

in selecting, rejecting, and simplifying what the camera sees. It is also the art of injecting emotional content into what could otherwise be a dull or ordinary picture, which evolves from the photographer's individual style and visual sense.

SUPPORT AND STABILITY

A composition must have a base upon which to rest, just as in nature. The pull of gravity draws everything to the earth. Unless we place a support under a flower pot such as a table or a window-ledge, for example, it obeys the law of gravitation and falls to the ground. To see a flower pot floating in mid-air or tilted at an extreme angle is, to say the least, contrary to natural law. Thus when a composition appears unstable or when it is tilted at an extreme angle, our visual senses revolt, and we refuse to accept it as normal or natural.

With this analogy we can understand that a head must not appear to be falling off its shoulders, or the figure inclined at a sharp angle as though it would lose balance and topple over. See Figures 63 and 64. Exceptions to this rule can be seen in Figures 65 and 66.

63. Tilting at a Sharp Angle   64. Corrected Angle

65. An Exception to the Rule

66. An Exception to the Rule

67. Inter-related Curves

INTER-RELATED CURVES

Nature is alive and continually in motion. Her atoms spin with inconceivable energy and rapidity and inter-acting curves creating form and motion. A single curve can be static and fail to convey this feeling. However, a sense of movement will be created by an inter-relation of curves.

The toy snake in Figure 67 furnishes an illustration of life and movement. As the snake crawls on its belly, its body assumes an inter-relation of curves. If we direct our eyes at one end of its body and follow the line of curves to the other end, we immediately get the feeling of actual movement; the snake looks alive. From this phenomenon of nature we have adopted the graceful "S" curve that we use in our arts. The application of this principle is shown in Figure 68.

In Figure 69, we have the same snake with only one curve. As we regard the snake here, we have the feeling of looking at something inanimate or dead.

Thus we borrow nature's key to all harmonious proportions of form and their expression of life and motion. The famous "S" curve is the line of beauty and grace that leads the eye in a pleasant manner along the continuity of its spiral line.

To further clarify this phenomenon of nature, let us digress for a moment, and discuss certain factors which are dependent upon the inter-relation of curves: If we observe the formation and motion patterns in nature—whether they are vegetable, animal, or for that matter, the patterns in our universe—we will notice a definite underlying composition that is similar to the formation and motion patterns of human anatomy. Because there is this similarity, we can logically reason that our compositional principle of line of action and interest must, necessarily, stem from these patterns and that any other viewpoint is unappealing to our esthetic senses.

Without plunging into a long discourse on geometric designs, let us discuss the scientific facts pertaining to a straight line, two parallel lines, an angle, and a curve.

Through direct or superficial observation, many people wrongly believe that motion in a straight line exists, or that two lines can be parallel to each

68. The "S" Curve

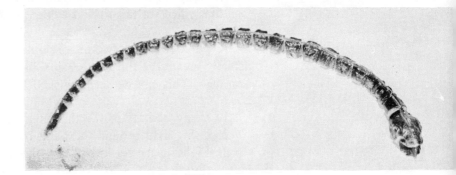

69. A Single Curve

other. Both beliefs are false. An examination of the facts proves that this observation is an optical illusion. If a straight line existed—even for a moment—the earth's gravitational pull would bend the line into a curve.

From one point of view, two lines can appear parallel to each other. But, here again it is an optical illusion. Two lines supposedly parallel to each other are automatically directed by gravitational pull to the center of the earth. According to the physical laws of gravity, the lines must, necessarily, form an angle.

It is now evident that we must form the following conclusions:

1. Because a line in motion is bent by gravitational pull into a curve, our visual senses are conditioned to curved body planes in motion. Any other pattern is usually unappealing.

2. No two body planes in motion can be parallel to each other, nor would they appear graceful if they were parallel.

3. No body planes in motion can form a sharp angle because a sharp angle is contrary to the physical laws of motion.

Having developed the fundamental ideas, let us prove them with illustrations:

Figure 70 illustrates a pose with straight and parallel body lines. Although the lines denote strength, they appear rigid and inanimate.

In Figure 71 the arms are contorted into angular lines. Although the lines convey a feeling of action, they lend the appearance of rigidity to the model.

In Figure 72 our main principle of line of action and interest is shown in its actual application. The body lines are curved and appear mutually connected and inter-related. The bends in the body curves do not form sharp angles. No two lines are straight, nor are there two lines parallel to each other. All in all, the figure appears graceful and appealing.

THE THIRD DIMENSION

Nature creates her compositions in a three-dimensional world with three-dimensional objects. So thoroughly ingrained is the sense of the third dimension that when we fail to find evidence of it in a photograph we are usually disturbed.

A photograph is two-dimensional. Although the photographer cannot actually create the third dimension in his photograph, he can create an illusion of it. This can be accomplished by:

1. Using accents in the distant areas.
2. Using light around the point of interest or directly back of it.
3. Lighting the subject so that the skin tones are delicate in their gradation.
4. Lighting with contrasts.
5. Lighting with shadows and highlights.

80

70. Straight and Parallel Lines

71. Angular Lines

72. Curved Body Lines

To sum up, the elements which make up composition are:

1. Focal (or dominating primary) point of interest.
2. Secondary (or supporting) point of interest.
3. Additional points of interest.
4. Location of the primary point of interest in the upper half of the frame.
5. Support and stabilization of the composition.
6. Direction of the figure into a plausible inter-relation of its curves.
7. Production of the illusion of a third-dimensional depth.

The focal point of interest is emphasized by contrast, or by being rendered either the brightest or the least illuminated area of the whole composition. The secondary and additional points of interest serve to support the theme by indicating motion and pantomime as well as mass, and by imparting a feeling of atmosphere, or mood.

We have established that space, depth, and distance around the focal point of interest in our composition are to be achieved by intelligent placement of the elements or ingredients. All these factors are an aid in binding the entire composition together as a unit telling a story.

We have dissected composition, brought it out into the open so that we may understand it, and have found that it is often related to many of the simple forms in nature.

Now we have a grasp of composition as it applies to our work and to the aspects of it known as "esthetic appeal". We are also able to analyze composition and distinguish whether it will please our senses or jar them. What is most important—we have established the reasons why.

7

Posing the Head and Shoulders

GOOD HEAD AND SHOULDER POSING DEPENDS FUNDAMENTALLY UPON THE angle of the head and its relation to the spinal column and the shoulders. Not only must this relationship be kept in mind, but the model should, at all times, be kept relaxed and comfortable.

Which brings to mind a good rule: The less the photographer manipulates the model's head the better. Too many attempts to direct it in this or that position will result in constriction and stiffness. Usually, if the model is comfortably posed, her head will assume a natural and characteristic pose. If, however, the model, as a matter of habit, carries her head inclined to one side, as in Figure 73, then of course, it requires correction.

One of the most common faults in posing the head is creation of strain by too sharp an angle between the head and the shoulders. While it is true that a pleasing sense of balance and motion is imparted by turning the head at a different angle to the shoulders, the head should not be turned too far on its axis. Invariably, the model's head and neck will appear strained (Figure 74).

Head and shoulders both at right angles or directly facing the camera will appear like a passport-type photograph—stilted and mechanical in appearance. The shoulders will appear massive. The pose, in general, will not depict motion or a sense of animation. Instead, it will appear static (Figure 75).

With the head posed facing the camera, and the body turned at an angle away from the camera, the pose will appear more pleasing (Figure 76). The photograph as a whole will convey a feeling of animation. Or we might say,

85

73. The Head Is Inclined to One Side

74. The Head Is Turned at a Sharp Angle

75. Head and Shoulders at Right Angles

76. The Body Is Turned at an Angle

"A sense of motion, in the sense that we can almost visualize that the subject's head was originally on the same plane as the shoulders were." The subject, however, just turned her head towards the camera when the shutter was tripped.

So far, from what we have learned, it is clear that when the head is posed facing the camera, the body should be turned at an angle or away from the camera. This rule is also indicated for all other poses. In short, The body should always be turned at a different angle than the head, no matter what type of pose is used.

There are three basic head and shoulder poses and infinite variations thereof. Since there are many variations, a full discussion would require more space than is at our disposal here.

THE THREE BASIC POSES ARE

1. Full-face view (face turned squarely towards camera).
2. Three-quarter face view (face turned forty-five degrees of the camera axis).
3. Profile view (face turned ninety degrees of the camera axis).

Full-Face View

Figure 77 illustrates a full-face view.

1. The face is turned squarely toward camera.
2. The body, sitting erect, is turned in the opposite direction from the head.
3. The arm nearest background extends far enough to lend a graceful base to the composition.
4. The hand nearest camera rests easily just along side body.

This, in essence, is a good composition of a full-faced view.

Figure 78 is a variation of the previous illustration insofar as we have added a feeling of motion by tilting the body towards the camera.

1. The model's left knee is crossed over her right knee.
2. The arm nearest background extends and rests on knee.
3. The body tilts towards the camera.
4. Subject's right hand rests on posing bench.
Figure 79 is another variation of a full-face view.

87

1. The body is tilted towards the subject's lap.
2. The left knee is crossed over the right one.
3. The arm nearest background extends and rests on the knee.
4. The arm nearest camera rests lightly at her side.

In this illustration a greater feeling of motion is imparted by the degree of body tilt towards the subject's knee.

Figure 80 illustrates still another variation of a full-face view.

1. The body sits erect and is turned almost ninety degrees of the camera axis.
2. The right knee is crossed over the left one.
3. The hand nearest camera extends and rests on knee.
4. Her other arm (arm nearest background) is straight down at her side and out of view.

Three-quarter Face View

Figure 81 illustrates a three-quarter face view.

1. Face is turned forty-five degrees of the camera axis.

77. The Full-Face View

78. Variation of the Full-Face View

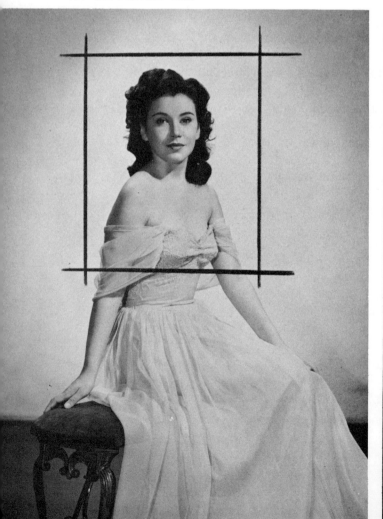

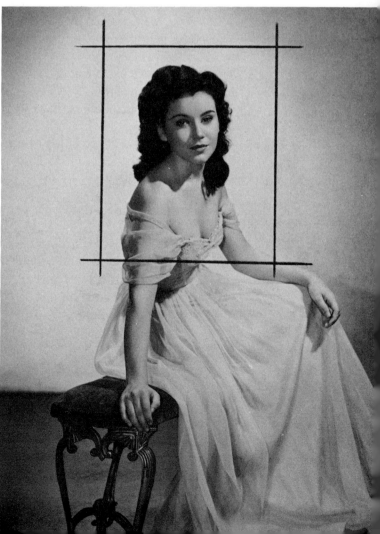

2. The body is turned almost squarely to camera.
3. Both hands extend and rest lightly at subject's*side.

Figure 82 illustrates a variation of a three-quarter face view.

1. In this pose the body faces the background at a forty-five degree angle and tilted in the direction of the subject's right side.
2. The hand nearest camera extends and rests on posing bench.
3. The hand nearest the background is straight down at her side—out of camera view.

Here again, a feeling of movement has been imparted by the diagonal tilt of the body.

Profile View

Figure 83 illustrates a profile view.

1. The face is turned ninety degrees of the camera axis.
2. The body is turned about thirty degrees of the camera axis.
3. Subject's right knee is crossed over her left one.
4. Her right arm rests on her knee.
5. Her left hand extends and rests on posing bench.

79. Variation of the Full-Face View   **80. Variation of the Full-Face View**

81. Three-quarter Face View   82. Variation of the Three-quarter Face View

Also notice the diagonal tilt of her shoulders.

Figure 84 is another profile view.

1. The body faces the background at a forty-five degree angle.
2. Both hands extend and rest on the posing bench.

You may have noticed that all of the illustrations in this series were executed from the right side of the subject's face. To pose the left side, reverse the directions given.

CORRECTIVE PROCEDURES

Eye Direction

As a general rule, eyes will appear more expressive when they are looking in the same direction that the head is facing. Stated in another way, the eyes

90

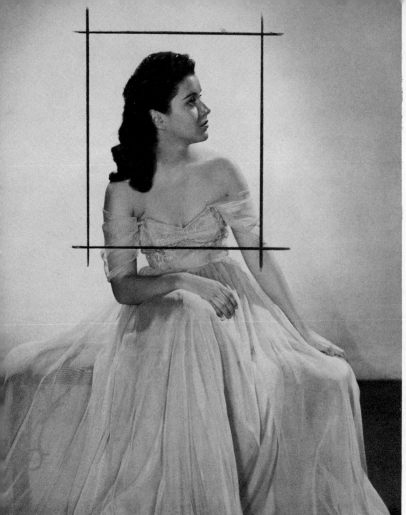

83. Profile View   **84. Variation of the Profile View**

should look in the same direction that the nose is pointing. Presenting the eyes in this manner is natural and usual in the course of daily experience.

There are, of course, exceptions to this rule, such as those used in the portrayal of mood interpretation, story illustration, and feminine expressions directly related to glamour photography.

When a person looks straight ahead (in the direction that the head is facing), the iris of the eye is located in the center of the eye socket. Coupled with this placement, the greatest point of eyelid opening is located in this central area. Because of this greater separation, it necessarily follows that directing the eyes so the iris is in the center of the eye socket will make the eyes appear larger and more expressive.

Photogenic Side of Face

Some photographers state that, by far, the majority of people photograph better from the left side of the face. Others claim that the right side is more

91

photogenic. And then again, still others say the photogenic side for women is on the full side of the hair (opposite the part).

Upon close observation of women's faces we would find that the nose is seldom in the exact center of the face, but usually is tilted to one side or the other. In many cases the photogenic side of the face is the side that the nose tilts towards.

However, when all is said and done, it is for you to analyze each one of your subjects and thus determine for yourself which side of the face is more photogenic.

Camera Angles

The camera angle in its relation to facial structure is an important aid as a corrective procedure. By making use of it we have the choice of perspective best suited to the subject's facial structure. With it we can also minimize facial faults.

Usually, the vantage point of the camera lens is at the subject's eye level. This level reveals a symmetrical face to its best advantage. There are, however, subjects whose features require a different angle.

To provide an understanding of camera angles, let us study the end result if we place the camera lens below the eye level of the subject:

1. The face will appear wider.
2. The forehead will be narrower.
3. The nose will appear shortened.
4. The nostrils will appear prominent, and distracting.
5. The jaw becomes more prominent.
6. The chin will appear longer.
7. The neck will become longer.

If we raise the level of the camera lens above the eye level of the subject:

1. The face will appear longer.
2. The forehead will become higher.
3. The nose will appear longer.
4. The jaw will be less prominent.
5. The chin will appear shorter.
6. The neck will appear shorter.

CORRECTIVE POSING

92

A face will appear slimmer turned at an angle away from the camera.

By turning the face to a three-quarter pose, its features will immediately appear narrow.

Tipping the head and shoulders towards the camera places the level of the jaw line down over the neck, thereby shortening a long neck.

Tipping the shoulders towards the camera and raising the head slightly will eliminate a double chin.

A long nose can be made to appear shorter by tipping the head up.

Lowered Chin

Your model may, at times, lower her chin after you have posed it at a correct level. You must, therefore, always be on the alert for this chin drop. If it occurs, direct your model to raise her head.

Posing the chin too low shortens the chin, lengthens the nose, and shortens the neck.

Raised Chin

Your model may also raise her chin after you have posed it at a correct level. Posing the chin too high fore-shortens the face, over emphasizes the nostrils, accents the jaw, makes the eyes appear smaller, and the neck longer.

Jutting Jaw

Sometimes a model will tend to tilt her jaw towards the camera, thus creating the appearance of a large jowl. Correct it by directing the model to tilt her jaw away from the camera.

Merging Facial Lines

In a three-quarter head pose, the nose may locate close to or beyond the cheek line. These angles produce a merging of facial lines and a bad presentation of the eye furthest from the camera. In a three-quarter head pose, a correct presentation locates the nose well within the area of the cheekline. The eye farthest from the camera will also look better.

Partial Profile

In effect, similar problems may arise in a profile pose. Distractive elements are created if (from the camera's point of view) we include any part of the far side of the face, the side farthest from the camera. The head should be turned at an angle away from the camera to a point where the far side of the face (as it is viewed from the angle of the camera) is not seen.

The general principles underlying the head and shoulder pose having been described, we will end this chapter with a discussion of a very important aspect of posing, namely, attention to detail.

Although you may be able to elicit good expressions and direct your models into good poses, your photographs can be disappointing because of some detail you overlooked while taking the sitting. I am referring to neatness of hair, neatness of clothing, neatness in all details.

The following details are those you should look for and correct at the time of the sitting:
1. Stray hairs and locks of hair
2. Wrinkles in clothing
3. Crooked necklace
4. Crooked neckline of dress

Check these details when you pose your model. Then view them from your camera. A detail that may appear perfect when you are posing your subject may appear wrong when viewed in the ground glass.

Stray hairs and locks of hair will probably cause you the most difficulty.

After posing your subject, view the effect from a distance (at an angle close to the camera lens) and check for gaps or stray locks of hair. In the event the hair needs adjustment, tuck in stray hairs and fill in gaps. Then go back to your camera again. If you then find that the hair is so disorderly that you cannot correct it, ask your model to fix it herself.

8
Posing the Figure

THE INFORMATION THAT WE HAVE ACQUIRED IN THE CHAPTER ON COMPOSI-
tional elements will be relatively easy to apply in posing the figure. We have
the knowledge of what elementary composition is, how it is constituted, and
its ingredients. We can take this information and apply it to posing the figure.
We must, however, realize that there are specific and recognizable faults in
posing the human body.

Moreover, we can be reasonably certain that if the model is left to her
own posing initiative (whether she is experienced or inexperienced), she
may assume any number of posing attitudes which will not appear well com-
posed either in isolated parts or in its entirety. These poor poses must be
known to us and avoided whenever possible.

Rather than follow a complex and multiple set of rigid rules, it is far
better to point up, with text and illustrations, the individual body areas as
either good or bad placement; in other words, discuss what is desirable,
what to avoid, and how a pleasing disposition of the body lines can be
secured. This, in essence, is the purpose of this chapter.

When the human figure is in a sitting or standing attitude, all of its
muscles and lines are pulled down by gravity. In a well arranged pose, the
body produces a counter force by balancing on its spinal column. Thus the
symmetrical form of the body is immediately improved. We can, therefore,
assume that the art of figure posing is based primarily on maintaining this
relationship between the spinal column and the various planes of the body.

In the nude, the body does not always appear natural in all poses depicting action. In our civilized condition, we usually assume that the body undressed and indoors is relaxed or at ease (Figure 85). Exceptions to this rule are dance poses, dynamic interpretations, or pictures taken outdoors in natural surroundings (Figure 86).

There are poses which look graceful when the model is clothed, yet appear awkward in the nude. This is largely due to the fact that the body, seen in the nude, and in certain attitudes, reveals many distortions of its planes, not apparent or distinguishable in the clothed figure. These distortions would be particularly emphasized with the model in relaxed positions posed in the nude.

Figure 87 shows the body in a slouched posture. The spinal column is collapsed. The abdomen is distended and tension is created in the upper arm, causing it to flatten into an unsightly mass of flesh. The outline of one of the breasts appears somewhat distorted and pendulous. Both legs are thrown out of proportion, one of them amputating the forearm. The entire effect is displeasing to the eye, causing it to wander from one unappealing body area to another without esthetic satisfaction.

Figure 88 is an example of a sagging spinal column which causes many other faults. Immediately apparent is the lack of pleasing proportions in the neck, shoulders, bust, and arms. The neck appears tightened and knotted. The shoulders are hunched and distorted, throwing the shape of the breasts out of proportion. One forearm appears foreshortened and emaciated. The extremity of one leg is cut off by a sharp angle that leaves a leg stump and a left-over toe placed meaninglessly above the other leg. The entire body appears to be sagging listlessly, without any of the pleasing proportions, vitality, or feeling of motion found in Figure 89.

Figure 90 illustrates an erample of muscular tension. Although the body position in itself is a relaxed and normal pose to assume, the muscles are tensed. We can almost feel the tension conveyed throughout the figure. Extreme muscle tension is usually undesirable, since it distorts the soft curves so pleasing in the female figure. There are times, however, when special requirements warrant the use of special methods. For the purposes of pantomime and dramatic interpretations, muscular tension is sometimes employed to create the illusion of greater movement or of emotion

The position of the feet has an important bearing upon the appearance of the entire body.

85. The Relaxed Pose Indoors

86. The Body in Motion Outdoors

87. A Slouched Posture

88. A Sagging Spinal Column

89. An Erect Spinal Column

90. Muscular Tension

In Figure 91 the placement of the feet automatically forces the entire body to become tensed in its struggle to maintain equilibrium. The feet appear as though they are about to move. However, if the weight of the body rests entirely on one foot, the other may be posed to form a graceful support for it as in figure 92. Here we have a culmination of intended motion. Moreover, there will be a relaxation of the muscles and a disposition of the body planes in the form of pleasing body curves.

Distortion results when any body joint is bent sharply, causing unsightly angles and the appearance of strain in the adjoining parts of the anatomy.

In Figure 93 the sharp bend in the knee creates the stump of a leg, as if the leg were cut off at that point. This is displeasing to the eye.

In Figure 94 distortions may be noticed in posing the arms. Here, stumps are created when the arms are bent sharply. In addition, the strained position of the arms created tension in other parts of the body. A more pleasing result is achieved when the arms are placed as in Figure 95.

Figure 96 again illustrates poor placement. In the nude figure, crossing one leg over the other creates unsightly lines and causes the muscles and tissues of adjoining parts of the body to become distorted. The leg over which the upper one is crossed appears cut off at the knee with a disjointed portion appearing beyond the other knee. Both thighs are distended and swollen out of proportion by the tension. And of course, these faults would not be evident in the clothed figure.

Figure 97 illustrates a pinching or creasing of the thigh. This is caused by too much extension of the upper part of the body, thereby placing excessive weight on the thigh.

In Figure 98 we have the result of having an arm extended too far from the body. This carries the eye away from the figure, and accents the large dark area between the body and the arm. Instead of being of secondary interest, the arm competes with the body in importance.

Figure 99 is an example of a beautiful pose spoiled by an extended arm. Here again the viewer's eye is directed away from the figure to the extended arm, causing a strong secondary point of interest.

In Figure 100 the arm seems to be collapsing under the weight of the body, attracting undue attention to the arm, and dividing interest between the bend in the arm and the rest of the body.

Figure 101 illustrates a good placement of the arm and hand.

In Figure 102 the poor placement of the arms has resulted in a darker tone in the far arm, creating a primary point of interest in an area of secondary importance. Furthermore, the arm appears growing out of the side of the body.

Figure 103 shows the removal of this fault by the simple procedure of eliminating the far arm from view.

91. Incorrect Placement of the Feet

92. Correct Placement of the Feet

93. Leg Stump

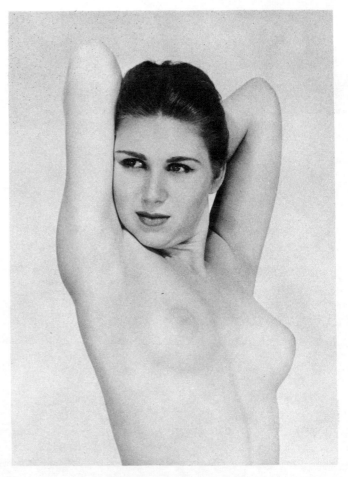

94. Arm Stump

95. A Correct Arm Placement

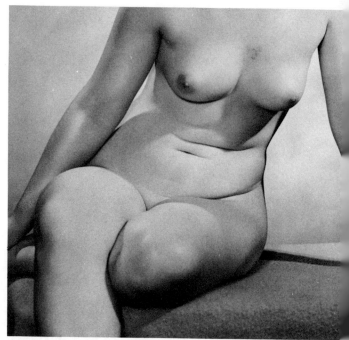

96. Crossing One Leg over the Other

97. Creasing the Thigh

98. Extended Arm

99. A Pose Spoiled by an Extended Arm

100. A Collapsing Arm

101. A Correct Placement of Arm and Hand

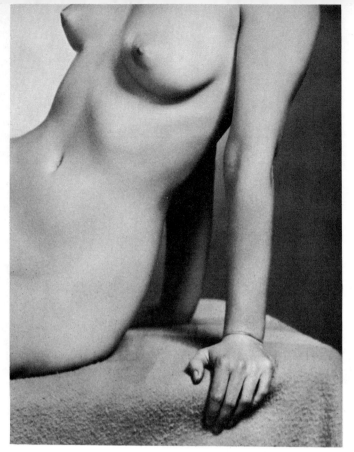

102. Partially Visible Arm

103. Corrected Arm Placement

Since there is no such thing as physical perfection in one female, you will inevitably encounter one or more structural faults in most of your models. No doubt, you will want to minimize these faults.

The art of corrective figure posing rests upon a fundamental principle of the phenomenon of perspective: A body area further away from the camera lens will appear smaller and less prominent. On the other hand, a body area closest to the camera lens will appear larger.

We can employ this formula as a corrective as follows:

To narrow a wide body structure, turn it at an angle to the camera.

To widen a very slim body structure, square it to the camera.

A small bustline will appear larger if it is turned at an angle or posed with the torso leaning towards the camera.

A large bustline will appear smaller if it is tilted away from the camera.

To narrow a wide hipline, turn it at an angle or pose it further away from the camera.

To widen a narrow hipline, square it full on or pose it closer to the camera.

Short legs will appear longer with a lens level lower than the waistline.

Heavy legs will appear slimmer if they are posed at an angle to the camera.

Slim legs will appear wider if they are squared to the camera in a standing pose or at an angle in a sitting pose.

INTERMEDIATE BODY ATTITUDES

Mediocrity in glamour photography is usually the companion of the photographer whose work is stilted by a sameness of style and technique, a procedure he usually applies to all women at random, regardless of their individual personality or other assets.

Although the center of interest in a glamour photograph is largely found in the portrayal of personality and facial expression, the tilt of the model's head, the graceful disposition of her hands, or the attitude of her figure, all play their part in capturing and revealing the individuality of the model.

We can usually recognize a model that we know well by her mannerism even though we may not see her face, because we are familiar with the way she walks, the way her hands express themselves, or other attitudes of her figure. All these serve to capture her character and personality. If these recognizable personality patterns are to be included in a photograph of her, we must give them their proper place and prominence.

Usually, the viewer's eye focuses on one body area at a time, and all

107

104. Variation on a Basic Pose

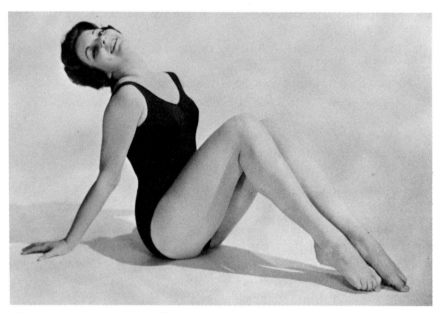

105. Variation on a Basic Pose

other areas are seen in a more or less impressionistic manner. This must not be taken to mean that, except for the model's face, her other assets should be classified as secondary points of interest—far from the truth. They all serve an important role in the characterization of the model's feminine qualities.

Among several variations of a pose, there is generally one which is outstanding in comparison to the others. If we stop and reason with this preference, we will find that there is something—perhaps an indefinable something —in the facial expression or the arrangement of the body lines that reveal or emphasize the most desirable characteristics of the model, or add grace and interest to the picture.

Figures 104 to 108 are variations on a basic pose and the author's choice.

After studying these photographs, we must agree that shooting several variations of a basic pose can serve to capture one pose and expression that is outstanding in comparison to the others.

106. Variation on a Basic Pose

107. Variation on a Basic Pose

108. The Author's Choice

 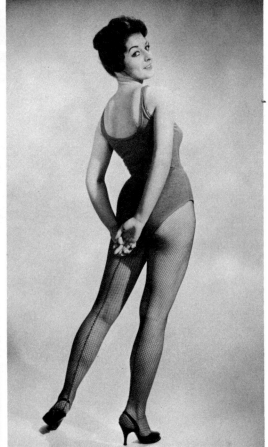

109. The Model Lets Herself Go   110. The Model Lets Herself Go

TEST SHOTS

The professional photographer is sometimes at a disadvantage getting a model for a specific need because he may see the model for the first time at the actual time of the sitting. Other than what he can see in her picture portfolio, he does not know anything about this girl. Under these circumstances there is little opportunity to study her photogenic qualities or her personality and posing ability. On the other hand, with the amateur photographer things are different; his models are generally girls with whose life and manner he is already familiar by association. Therefore, in the event the model is not known, it is worthwhile to make a series of test shots wherein

111. The Model Lets Herself Go   112. The Model Lets Herself Go

the model can express and reveal those little details of her personality, figure, and posing attitudes.

Figures 109 to 112 are part of a series of test shots which were taken after the model was instructed to let herself go, so to speak, without specific instructions or direction.

As we can see, these photographs definitely reveal the girl's charm, pleasing personality, and her adaptability to variations in posing. Thus we are assured that with proper direction, a good model can execute a versatile range of good posing patterns and facial expression.

111

9
Facial Expression

IT IS FACIAL EXPRESSIVENESS THAT ADDS INTEREST TO A PHOTOGRAPH. IT helps sell about 95% of all formal portraiture. Your work may be of the highest order, technically speaking, but it will fall on its face if your photographs are devoid of expression. On the other hand, a photograph may lack quality and yet be interesting because it has expression. Expression is to a photograph what color is to a painting. It adds the warmth of human feeling and the reality of life.

In recent years experimental psychology has taught us a great deal about human emotions and the facial expressions they produce. Most of this data is of value to us, for if we know the make-up of an emotion, we may produce with predetermined accuracy the stimuli required to bring about a desired expression.

If it were possible for us to duplicate under experimental laboratory control the conditions of a sitting, we would conduct the experiment in very much the same manner as other psychological tests. We would place the subject under observation and note his emotional reactions to various stimuli. At the conclusion of the experiment, we would know some of the responses produced by each stimulus.

Although this example of what could take place under controlled conditions is purely hypothetical, it does serve to illustrate the need for such information. For this knowledge is not available to the student of photography, either in the classroom or in text books on photography. It may be found, however, in modern text books on psychology. For, although you cannot learn to activate the emotions simply by reading about their char-

113

acteristics, it is quite possible to learn the nature of their responses.

Psychologists tell us that emotional motivation in a normal person usually can be traced to internal or external stimuli. Somewhere in the conditions of his environment, they say, there are pleasant or annoying factors that are registered by the nerves, and are then carried as impressions to the brain. These impressions are activated by the sense of sight, smell, touch, and hearing. The reaction to a stimuli may be immediate and automatic, or modified, according to the person's degree of self-control.

Such reactions are most frequently automatic reflexes and, as such, are relatively simple because of their involuntary nature. Far more complicated is the habit pattern that is built up during a lifetime of meeting outside situations. If these habit patterns of the human being are activated purely in an automatic manner—as they are in simpler organisms—the behavior of the subject under known conditions could easily be predicted. But there is a far more involved pattern of reaction in the human organism, namely, the motivations that arise out of the memory and thought processes. As a person grows older, his memory acquires a store of experiences; consequently, it is ever-ready to present the mind with a known pattern of reaction. These patterns become more and more set until, in the adult, there is an automatic reaction to conditions as they arise.

To illustrate, a person may be adversely affected by the most innocuous outside stimuli, such as the aseptic odor of a dentist's office or the sight of a photographer's camera. Both stimuli in themselves are harmless, but they may be so inter-related with the person's habit patterns of thinking and with his past experiences that they may be sufficient in themselves to set up in the mind adverse associations that give rise to fear.

In view of the diversity of these factors, it is manifestly impossible for anyone to know the exact conditions necessary to engender fear or happiness, for no such broad pattern of responses exists. You should keep in mind, though, that the response of the subject will depend to a great extent upon the habit patterns set up in her mind. You cannot, nor need you try to uncover her thoughts and habits. You must be observant enough, however, to detect the earliest symptoms of their emotional expression, and introduce factors that will elicit favorable responses.

In short, a specific expression may be elicited by activating the subject's emotional responses in the knowledge that she will react to the stimulation out of past experience.

The various emotional states of a human being can be observed by the changes that take place in the muscular structure of the face. Patterns thus created reflect the person's reactions to his environment, and are universally recognized symbols of inner emotions. In other words, these patterns, in

114

most cases, represent a visual picture of the feeling being experienced by the subject.

There is a great range of expressions with many variations, especially about the mouth and in the upper facial muscle groups. A muscle contraction induced by mental associations of pleasure or amusement draw the corners of the mouth upward and produce a gentle smile (Figure 113). When the impulse is deepened, the mouth opens and the teeth show (Figure 114). The versatility of the group of muscles around the eyes adds greatly to the expression. Some lift the brow and wrinkle the forehead cross-wise to produce an expression of surprise (Figure 115). Other muscles draw the brow together and wrinkle the center of the forehead vertically when a person feels displeasure or pain (Figure 116).

Although the muscles of the mouth are more expressive than those of the eyes, both muscle groups usually are coordinated in an expression. There are, of course, exceptions. For example, there are people who cannot smile convincingly, no matter how they try. Their eyes remain expressionless.

In Figure 117, the mouth appears to smile while the eyes remain dull and expressionless.

Figure 118 illustrates coordination of both muscle groups. If you cover the mouth in both illustrations, the difference in the expression of the eyes becomes apparent.

We can divide the gamut of expressions into two classifications: those that are useful to the glamour photographer and those that are not. Our task consists of isolating and portraying the attractive aspects of expressions.

113. A Pleasant Expression

114. A Smile

115. Surprise

116. Pain

117. The Eyes Appear Dull

118. Coordination of the Mouth and Eyes

In every expression there are many levels of intensity. As a mood builds up, there are several recognizable stages prior to the culmination of that particular expression.

Similarly, after a mood has reached its peak, several anti-climactic levels are apparent as the expression recedes. In both these phases, some of the stages of the expression are not suitable for glamour photography, because they appear either weak or false and tend to annoy after they have been viewed for a while.

We can clarify this by narrowing the patterns of emotional expressions to those that are suitable for our use.

Let us study the series of expressions in Figure 119 to 126, inclusive. In each photograph there is an intensification of the expression from a stare to unrestrained laughter.

Not all of these expressions are useful to us. Figure 119, features an inanimate or blank expression, not the least bit attractive. This photograph illustrates the lack of coordination so frequently encountered at the outset of a sitting. The photographer has not been able to condition the subject's responses.

In Figure 120, the eyes have an expression of interest. Although the expression is not a pleasant one, it is appealing.

In Figure 121, good coordination between the muscles of the mouth and the eyes has resulted in a pleasant expression.

Figure 122 features a smile that would be well correlated except that, with the mouth closed, the extension of the smile produces a distorted mouth.

Figure 123 clearly illustrates the inadvisability of using expressions that are neither of one kind nor the other. If you intend to portray an unrestrained smile, you should seek to capture that mood with a coordination of the mouth and eyes. In this illustration the mouth is slightly open, revealing just a portion of the teeth. The expression appears as though it started towards fullfillment but never reached it. It is not an attractive smile.

Figure 124 represents an ideal blending of the factors that combine to produce a natural smile with the teeth showing.

Figure 125 and 126, are examples of anti-climactic smile reactions.

In Figure 125, the smile has built up to the point where the lower teeth show. When this occurs, the smile is out of control, and the expression is not suitable.

In Figure 126, the exuberance of the expression has gone to such an extreme that it gives the viewer an uneasy and agitated feeling. However, this expression can be effectively used in story illustration, and in indoor and outdoor glamour photography.

The unattractive emotional expressions, such as anger, fear, hate, and sorrow, despite being unattractive, nevertheless, do have a specific place

117

119. A Blank Expression

120. An Expression of Interest

123. A Border-line Expression

124. A Natural Smile

121. A Pleasant Expression

122. Distorted Mouth

125. Lower Teeth Showing

126. Over-Exuberant Smile

127. Story Illustration

128. Story Illustration

and purpose. These expressions are used almost exclusively in theatrical and illustrative story photography as an aid to conveying pantomimic symbols of emotional states.

Figures 127 to 134 are illustrative story interpretations. Here specific emotions were elicited by activating the emotional responses in the knowledge that the subjects would react to the stimulation out of past experiences.

Now the question arises, "How is this accomplished?" The answer is based on the photographer's ability as a director. This ability encompasses the coordination of a great many factors, such as, his personality qualifications, his intellectual and emotional nature, his knowledge of human relations, his camera room manner—his directing technique.

129. Story Illustration

130. Story Illustration

131. Story Illustration

132. Story Illustration

133. Story Illustration

134. Story Illustration

10

Lighting Arrangements

GOOD LIGHTING TAKES INTO ACCOUNT THE PERFECTIONS AND IMPERFECTIONS of the model, and seeks to subdue the imperfections into lower light tones, while at the same time searching out and highlighting the beauty of her face and form in whatever way the sensibilities of the photographer demands. Whether this lighting is done in high key or low key, whether he develops an affinity for a particular style that stamps him as an individualist, whether his work tends to be stereotyped, or expresses his ability in a wide range of techniques, remains his decision. We must keep in mind that the art of lighting affords an unlimited opportunity for creative expression and that it is as varied as the personality and skill of the photographer.

However, whether the photographer works in high or low key, whether he is greatly advanced in the art of lighting or a relative beginner, there is one thing he must not forget: If he approaches the subject of lighting carelessly, though he may have the best of intentions, he will fall far short of satisfactory results. The human eye and mind is such that unless careful attention is given, the beauty of the model will go unnoticed. He must study his subject minutely, paying close attention to the details of form and structure. He must be careful even of the smallest shadows which his lights create. In his effort to paint with light, he must always seek to bring out the very best. By this studied concentration, the ultimate possibilities of his model will emerge, and he will see her beauty realized in his work.

The techniques of lighting are not difficult if we adhere and condition our minds to the basic principles of outdoor lighting. In other words, if we duplicate the phenomenon of light as it exists on our planet, we can produce

123

a wide range of lighting styles that are appealing to our visual senses.

In the execution of these methods, we will consider the light of the sun as a directional and highlighting medium that varies its light pattern upon the subject in relation to its position in the sky and the subject. We will call this concentrated illumination the "Modeling Light." The sky is another light source. It produces a soft, even, and over-all illumination that fills the entire picture area with light. We will designate the light of the sky as "Fill-in Light."

THE FILL-IN LIGHT

Since the fill-in light provides the necessary illumination to fill every part of the subject and record its details on our film, we will place the fill-in light as close to the camera as possible and at a height that is level with the center of the subject area. Once the light has been placed properly, forget about it and devote your attention to other details of the work. Your only return to it will be to vary its intensity either by moving it nearer to the subject or farther away. You must remember that it is always present with varied intensity and its position is always as close to the camera as possible, on that side of the camera which is farthest away from the modeling light. For example, if the modeling light is to be placed on the right-hand side of the camera, the fill-in light should be placed on the left-hand side of the camera and vice-versa.

Now let us discuss the exceptions to this rule: When using a short focal length lens, the subsequent short distance between camera and subject requires placement of the fill light nearer to the subject, if you are to keep the light unit close to the camera. This shorter distance concentrates the light rays into a narrow area, creating shadow pockets. In other words, the closer the fill light is to the subject, the greater the tendency to cause shadow pockets.

Shadow pockets may also occur in a close-up shot with the subject posed at a forty-five or ninety degree angle off the axis of the camera. If this difficulty arises, place the fill-in light on the same side with the modeling light—again, as close to the camera as possible. To further alleviate this problem, two fill-in lights may be used, one on each side of the camera.

In Figure 135A and its diagram, you can see for yourself exactly what happens when a photograph is recorded by the illumination of the fill-in light only. Observe that the record made of the subject is without drama or interest. It is as if we were seeing only with one eye, and with very little of the interest and attention which usually accompanies our sight outdoors in natural daylight. The photograph does not record a good representation of roundness and structure. It appears flat, with very little relief or depth. It

124

135A. Illumination of the Fall-in Light

135B. Diagram

lacks visual interest and therefore does not reflect a photographer's effort to produce an artistic result.

THE MODELING LIGHT

Our eyes can distinguish contours in relief only because of tonal differences—shadows and highlights. Although we can record tonal differences with the fill-in alone, it does not, used by itself, produce a full tonal scale or brilliant highlights. Basically, a full tonal range and brilliant highlights are produced by adding a modeling light.

Figure 136A and its diagram reveal the effect of adding a modeling light to the previous illustration. Interest is heightened by introducing highlights and accents. The roundness of the form is now dramatically registered.

125

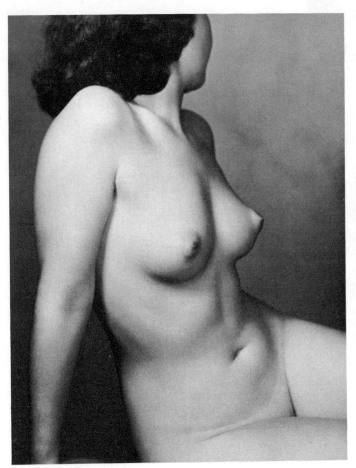

136A. Adding a Modeling Light

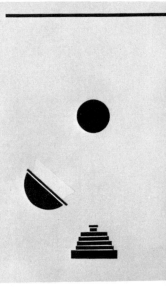

136B. Diagram

BACKGROUND LIGHT

The background light creates a feeling of atmosphere and dimensional depth between the background and the subject. By lighting a broad or controlled area on the background, the subject is set away from it, guiding the viewer's eye to the focal point of interest.

Figure 137A and its diagram show the addition of the background light to the aforementioned lights. As we can see, the background light separates the figure from the background, creating an illusion of third dimension and accents to the outline of the form. Also the background light removes the drab looking background area which, in the previous illustrations, seem to swallow the figures into itself, and prevents it from standing out.

The time has come for us to relax our concentration upon the fundamentals of glamour photography. In the following illustrations you will find the simplest possible explanations and illustrations of lighting arrangements

126

137A. Adding a Background Light

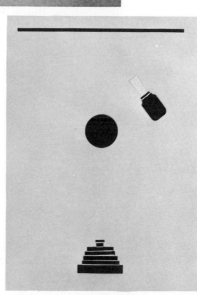

137B. Diagram

that the author has used to produce the finished illustrations in this work. You will not be distracted by the presence of an animate model, nor will you be oppressed by wordy explanations or marginal discussions. The pictures and diagrams will be instantly understandable and the text will deal only with facts which are pertinent to the immediate subject.

FRONT LIGHTING

Study Figure 138A and its diagram. The modeling light is placed close to the camera and elevated at a forty-five-degree angle to the manikin.

The fill-in light is placed on the opposite side of the modeling light, as close to the camera as possible and level with the central area of the figure.

The lighted background aids in the illusion of third dimension.

Notice that this lighting style produces a wide band of illumination with very little differentiation between light and shade.

FORTY-FIVE-DEGREE LIGHTING

Study Figure 139A and its diagram. The modeling light is rotated approximately forty-five degrees off the camera axis and elevated at a forty-five-degree angle to the manikin.

The fill-in light is placed on the opposite side of the modeling light as close to the camera as possible and level with the central area of the figure.

Here again the lighted background aids in the illusion of third dimension.

Also, deliniation of light and shade is more pronounced than in the front-lighting style. Separation of the tonal planes of the figure produce better modeling and increase the third-dimensional effect.

Figure 140 shows the effect produced with the modeling light placed at a forty-five degree angle and a strong fill-in light. The result brings out detail in the shadow areas, adding the appearance of weight to the figure.

Figure 141 shows the effect produced with the same lighting, but with a lower intensity fill-in illumination, resulting in deeper shadows, more distant plane separation, and narrowing of the figure.

Figure 142 illustrates a forty-five-degree modeling light and a fill-in light illuminating the muscular planes of the back.

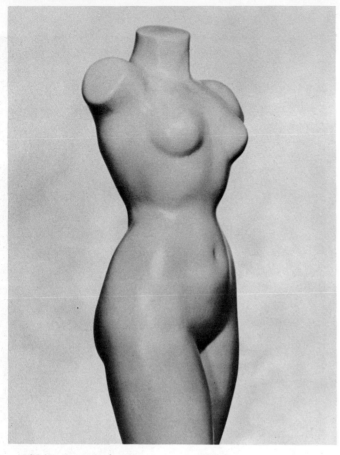

138A. Front Lighting

138B. Diagram

139A. Forty-five Degree Lighting

139B. Diagram

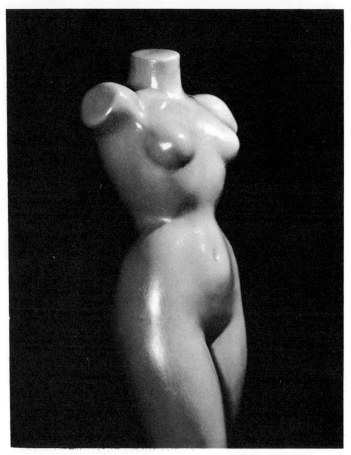

140. A Well Balanced Fill-in and Highlight Illumination

141. Low Intensity Fill-in Illumination

142. Lighting the Muscular Planes of the Back

Back-lighting is the best means of producing the illusion of third dimensional depth and brilliancy. Properly used, back-lighting produces definite separation between the subject and the background, separates the various body planes into strong relief, and creates an illusion of roundness and depth.

One Back-Light

Figure 143A and its diagram illustrate a spot light placed behind, slightly to the side (135 degrees off the axis of the camera) and elevated forty-five to sixty degrees to the figure. It should then be directed towards the figure at an angle to the camera. Make sure that you pivot the light unit on its axis so that its light does not strike the camera lens and cause flare.

Here, the intensity of the fill-in light is lower than with other lighting styles.

Figure 144 shows one back light and a fill-in illuminating the planes of the back.

Two Back-Lights

Figure 145A and its diagram illustrate two-back lights modeling both sides of the figure. The addition of a fill-in light reveals detail in the shadows. Here again, we must be careful to pivot the back-light units so the illumination does not strike the camera lens.

Figure 146 shows two back lights and a fill-in illuminating the planes of the back.

LIGHT RATIO

To obtain a proper and predetermined balance or ratio of light between the modeling light and the fill-in light, use the following procedure:

1. Place the fill-in light close to the camera.
2. Carefully study the highlight and shadow areas of the face or figure.
3. Move the fill-in light back, foreward, or "feathered" to the side.
4. When the shadow areas appear of about the right density, brighten them up a little more.

Explanation: This procedure will insure the required fill-in illumination, because black and white or, for that matter, color film, record shadows a little darker than the human eye sees them.

131

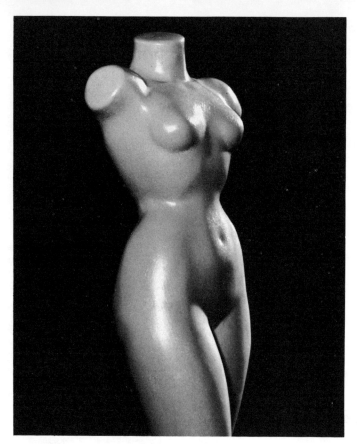

143A. One Back Light and a Fill-in

143B. Diagram

144. One Back Light and a Fill-in Illuminating the Planes of the Back

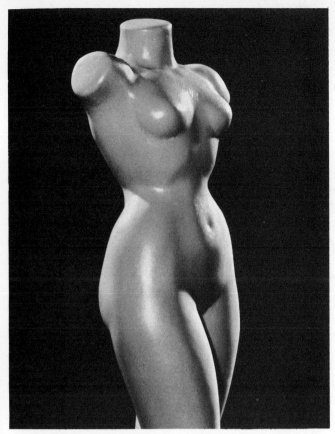

145A. Two Back Lights and a Fill-in

145B. Diagram

146. Two Back Lights and a Fill-in Illuminating the Planes of the Back

Backgrounds are basically a matter of personal taste and creative expression. However, we must take into consideration that interest needs to be concentrated on the subject—not the background. Therefore, avoid strong background designs and patterns, unless they are specifically related to the subject or location. Also, avoid drapes producing strong highlights and shadow patterns which call attention to themselves.

Background materials are again a matter of personal choice. Recommendations: Plain painted walls of light or medium tone, unbleached muslin, or similar materials used on a stretcher frame. No-seam paper background may also be used. Colors: Flat white, flat gray, or flat black.

In addition, remember that light, airy, and youthful interpretations are best produced with light color backgrounds. On the other hand, character, dramatic, or somber studies are more suitable with dark backgrounds.

INTERPRETATIONS

Figure 147, placed against a dark background, is shadowy, illusive, and well rounded, but confined dimensionally to narrow limits. It does not extend into any appreciable distance; it blends into the background. In this illustration we depend upon the delicate skin gradation to give it a third dimensional illusion.

The lighting in this instance was kept low, recording just enough on the negative to register every bit of detail in low key.

A model often possesses a striking anatomical feature. The photographer's attention will be captured, and his imagination will be fired to dramatize that feature against a dark background.

Figure 148 is such an illustration. The model's breasts are made a dominant point of interest by the correct use of back lights that mould the three-dimensional form. The full curve of the breasts are dramatically balanced against the tones of the arms. The use of back lights, adds roundness to the structure of the breasts. Here is an instance of light used to create a perfection in the model which could only be brought out through careful placement of this back lighting. The roundness and dimensions of the breast are suggested and emphasized by these lights. The restrained use of the fill-in light helps to subordinate the outline of the model's form. Here the breasts are made the dominant point of interest, and their beauty has impelled the author to restrain all other details by painting with light into a lower tone. The subtle contours of the abdomen are made to support the breasts, without drawing undue attention to this part of the anatomy.

134   The human figure is so finely balanced that we are often unaware of the

147. Narrow Limits of Dimensional Depth

muscular structure which is necessary to support the spine and maintain the body's balance. In Figure 149 the various muscular planes of the back are lighted against a dark background so as to maintain interest in the large area of the back which, in itself, is plain and lacking in interest. Whether you solve the problems involved in photographing the back of the figure by ignoring them, or you approach the problem bravely and achieve many beautiful effects, remains your decision.

A keynote of simplicity is struck in Figure 150. Gone is the plan for perfect organization of light and shadow. Gone is the precision of pose and pattern. Gone are the careful separation of planes and the anatomic perfection of breast, or thigh, or hip. Instead, we have a simple tactile warmth of feeling, the sensation of flesh touching flesh. Here is the simple repose of a model at ease, the interesting lift and fall of her arms and legs, and the bent back. How shall we explain such a digression from the orderly pattern of our thoughts? How shall we rationalize the fact that despite the many obvious shortcomings, the illustration is entirely satisfactory and capable of conveying all the beauty, softness, delicacy and elusive femininity which is the aim of our art to produce? The highlight upon the shoulder and back draws the eye to that area, which is certainly not of greatest interest or importance; and yet, if it were to be changed, the result would not be an improvement. This is a pose that was caught during a moment of rest. In terms of actual planning it is without forethought or purpose, but the interesting design of its many lines is such that even its shortcomings may be overlooked because it engenders a mood of repose and simplicity.

LOW KEY

If we study a scale of tones most commonly used in an esthetically appealing photograph, we would probably find a range from deep black to pure white, together with a full range of intermediate half-tones. This is called "a full scale print."

On the other hand, a low key photograph contains a predominance of dark tones ranging from deepest black to approximately the middle of the gray scale. There will be a few accenting highlights here and there to add a feeling of depth and brilliancy. In essence, low key photography is ideally suited for character, dramatic, somber, and so-called interpretive mood studies (Figure 151).

Low key is achieved by proper selection of subject matter, background, lighting, and film development. The negative possesses a delicate skin-tone gradation as well as a certain amount of contrast to lend a strong and forceful presentation of the subject. It also appears a little thinner than normal.

136

148. A Striking Anatomical Feature

149. The Planes of the Back

150. A Keynote of Simplicity

151. Low Key Interpretation

In most instances, the shadow areas are registered in perceptible detail, and in other cases, they may disappear into total inky blackness.

The author's method of producing a low key negative is as follows:

1. Illuminate and balance the shadows and highlights.
2. Expose the film slightly less than the film manufacturer's recommended A.S.A. rating.
3. Process the film longer than normal, with a diluted developer.

To add brilliancy and sufficient contrast to a thin or translucent negative, we can resort to a longer-than-normal development of the film. An inherent characteristic of black and white film is that the longer it is developed, the more the contrast is build up. Thus, if the film is slightly under-exposed at the start, we can still register plenty of gradation in the skin tones of our subject by means of longer development. If we wish to carry it a step further, we can also add more contrast and brilliancy by using a higher contrast paper. The personal taste and judgment of each individual photographer, based on prior experience, preferences, and experimentation will be the deciding factor here.

You may think that experimenting by trial and error in order to determine the best film exposure under your particular working conditions, is a long, time-consuming procedure. Not necessarily. A few trial and error experiments can be relatively short, and if you keep an accurate record throughout, they will provide everything you need for future reference.

HIGH KEY

Whereas low key photography contains a predominance of tones ranging from black to the middle tones of the gray scale, with a few highlights here and there to add brilliancy, the tonal make-up of a high-key interpretation is exactly the opposite. There is a predominance of light tones ranging from almost white to the middle tones of the gray scale (or even a complete absence of middle tones sometimes), but containing a few dark tones here and there.

Essentially, a good semi-high key or high key photograph contains either a very light and delicate gradation of skin tones or an almost complete omission of skin texture and middle tones. At the same time, it will have a two-dimensional line drawing effect along the outer edge of the subject (Figure 152).

As we can see, the mood is in a lighter vein. Therefore, it does not lend itself to so-called character or dramatic studies.

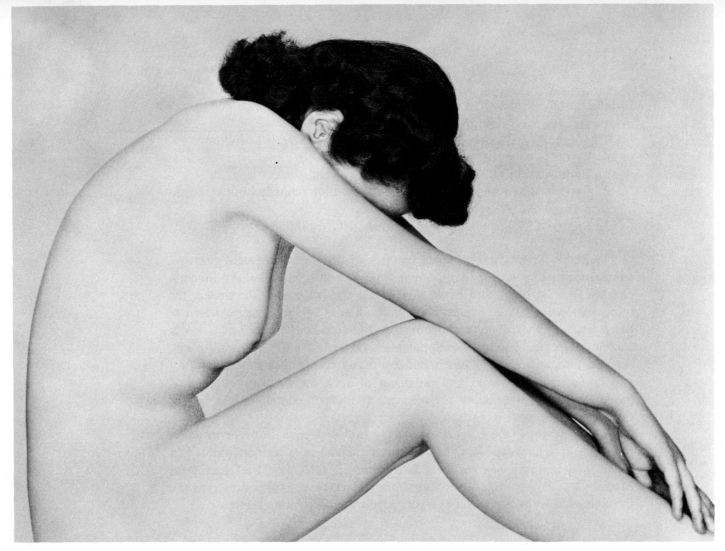

152. High Key Interpretation

As far as lighting techniques for high key are concerned, the approach is a comparatively simple one: any lighting style may be employed, providing the shadow areas are made very light. This is accomplished by using a fill-in light that will record shadow areas almost as bright as the modeling light. To facilitate matters, two fill-in lights may be used—one on each side of the camera.

STAGE LIGHTING

Stage lighting is not a natural lighting. Essentially, it is an outgrowth of theatre lighting. It is used primarily for grotesque and somber interpretations, as well for certain emotional expressions (anger, fear, hate, sorrow, etc.). Despite its being unattractive and therefore of doubtful value in glamour photography, stage lighting does have a specific place and purpose in theatrical and illustrative or story-telling photography.

Study Figure 153. The modeling light is directed up towards the subject's forehead from a low angle, directly in front of and close to the subject.

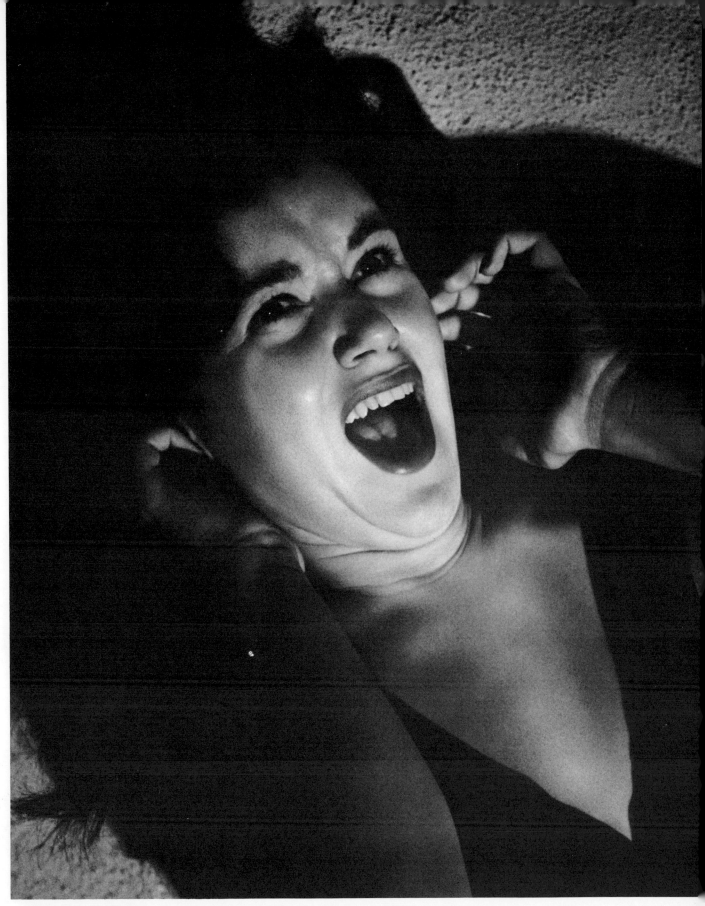

153. Stage Lighting

A fill-in light is placed close to the camera, level with the lens. Back lights may also be added to the set-up.

THE FILM

Outside of certain specifications such as speed or exposure latitude, there does not seem to be any appreciable difference between one film and another. Most modern films are good and they can be used with confidence. Select a film whose specifications meet your particular needs—then stick with it and learn all there is to know about it.

Film Speed

In the choice of film speed we must consider:
1. The intensity of the illumination to be used.
2. The f/stop required to gain sufficient depth of field.
3. The minimum shutter speed required to "freeze" subject motion.
4. An exposure that will produce a proper density level for a given degree of development.

Film Types

The panchromatic materials of today are sensitive to all visual colors and fairly accurate in the rendition of colors in tones of gray. However, panchromatic films do vary somewhat in their sensitivity to blue, green, and red. Panchromatic emulsions which are designated as type *B* are relatively high in green sensitivity. Type *C* emulsions are relatively high in red sensitivity.

Considering these sensitivity classes and their effect upon flesh tone rendition, type *C* emulsions, when used with tungsten lights with a color temperature which is less than 3,200° Kelvin have a tendency to overcorrect in the red of the spectrum. Therefore, type *B* panchromatic emulsions are to be considered for our purposes because they yield the most accurate flesh tones.

Exposure Determination

Although film manufacturers furnish A.S.A. (American Standards Association) exposure indexes which indicate the approximate light sensitivity for a given film, it must be remembered that other factors will influence speed values: type of processing, degree of contrast desired, and the purposes for which the negative is to be used. Where the rendition of good skin-tone values is important, the next lower speed index of a light-meter reading and

144

longer film development may often yield better results. A series of trial and error tests will enable you to ascertain the best results for a given film emulsion.

To the student experimenting by trial and error, a great deal of experimentation may be required if he approaches his work haphazardly, without aim or purpose. But if he will pose his model and place his lights in what he considers a proper balance, his next steps can be relatively short and extremely accurate:

Make several exposures of the same pose.

Expose at the manufacturer's rated film speed.

Deliberately expose *under* the rated speed, making two or three negatives and giving them each a different exposure time.

Now expose *over* the rated speed, again making two or three negatives and giving them each a different exposure time.

Identify each negative with its exposure time.

Finally, fully develop all the negatives.

You should then make prints from your chosen paper. The negative producing the best print will have been properly exposed.

Lighting Equipment

It is axiomatic among some photographers that the least number of lights used, the better the results. Some photographers work with a modeling light and a fill-in light to lighten the shadows. There are others who use a modeling light along with a reflector so placed that the light is reflected back into the shadows. Another prevailing opinion is: To achieve outline, accents, and third-dimensional depth, multiple lighting has to be employed. Despite these diversified approaches to lighting, we need not quarrel with either method. In the final analysis, it is not the number of lights used that determines the quality of a photograph, but *how* they are used. It, therefore, seems reasonable to conclude that a good photograph remains a good photograph in any lighting interpretation, whether we use one light, five lights, or for that matter, improvise with lights that were not specifically designed for photographic use.

An example of improvisation can be seen in Figure 154. This picture was taken by the author at night with available room light, a 100 watt reading lamp as a modeling light, a 60 watt reading lamp as a fill-in light, *Tri X* film, lens opening f3.5, and Exposure at 1/10 of a second.

We may conclude that, whether we acquire expensive lighting equipment or decide to buy within the medium or low priced range, the same qualitative results can be achieved. Our knowledge of good lighting techniques is more important than the quality of the lighting units.

154. An Example of Improvisation

It is not the author's intention to recommend the products of specific manufacturers. The lighting units described are simply specifications for your guidance and a basis for your choice of equipment. Specifications and performance adaptability are what count, rather than manufacturers's names.

If you prefer to start with inexpensive equipment, there are moderate and low priced lights on the market, reasonably well constructed, that can be expected to serve their purpose adequately. In fact, a good feature of the lower priced unit is its inherent light weight and portability.

Of course, if you possess ample means and you intend to furnish a well-equipped camera room, it is advisable that you purchase better lighting units that feature sturdiness, mobility, and smoothly moving parts.

In any event, a good rule to adopt is to buy the equipment of well-known manufacturers whose years of supplying the demands of the trade usually results in the development of efficient lighting units.

The Flood Light

A properly designed flood light has a parabolic reflector and is fitted on an adjustable stand. The lamp house has a tilting arrangement which pro-

146

vides a good range of angles in which the light may be directed. An attachable diffuser should also be provided. The light unit should be able to project a broad, even illumination. A flood light can be used as a modeling light or as a fill-in light.

The Spot Light

A spot light is a light source that concentrates the light rays into a narrow beam of illumination. A special type of spot light is equipped with a Fresnel lens. This consists of a small central plano-convex lens surrounded by a series of prismatic rings. This produces a strong light, but with a soft indistinct edge. Since the light rays from a spot light travel in near straight-line directions, the shadows cast have sharper defined edges than those produced by a flood light. The lamphouse should have a tilting arrangement which provides a good range of angles in which the light may be directed. The lamp house should also project an even field of illumination from a narrow beam to a broad field of light with a total absence of filament distortion or rings in the light field.

It is also important that the spotlight be provided with "barn doors." The barn doors are used tot control and shield the light beams. The doors may be opened to cut light at a desired angle, for confining to a desired place, and for keeping stray light from the camera lens and background.

Although a spotlight may be used as a modeling light for any of the lighting arrangements herein described, its greatest effectiveness seems to be as a backlight. Here the spotlight is ideal because its light can be confined by adjusting its barn doors.

A spotlight can also be used as a background light. The unit produces a circular pattern with a soft indistinct edge which can be controlled from a narrow beam to a broad field.

11

Outdoor Photography

IN THE LAST CHAPTER WE DISCUSSED THE PHENOMENON OF LIGHT AS IT exists in nature: The sun, projecting a directional and point source of light, falls upon the subject at an angle, and the variations in the position of the sun create interesting light patterns. Also, the light from the sky adds an even, frontal and overhead illumination. What we have learned about lighting can also be applied to outdoor photography, because the general principles that underlie indoor and outdoor lighting are basically the same.

OUTDOOR LIGHTING CONTRASTS

The intensity of light from the sun is relatively constant, whereas the light from the sky varies in proportion to the presence or absence of clouds and atmospheric haze. For example, On a very clear day when the sky is a deep blue, the ratio of light between the sun and the sky is approximately 7:1 (Figure 155).

As we can see, here we have extremes of light and shade, with the end result that the skin shadows are hardly discernible.

When the sky is completely overcast and the sun is hidden by a blanket of dense clouds, the light falling upon the subject is mostly that of the sky's diffused light. The illumination is almost uniform over most of the subject (Figure 156). Here, the picture lacks contrast.

Figure 157 illustrates a well balanced ratio of light and shade (sun and sky). The sun is at an angle, lending crisp highlights to the figure while the shadows are registered in detail.

Since we will encounter a different contrast range for various outdoor

148

lighting conditions, we must be aware that the ratio of highlight and shadow is governed by variations in light conditions such as prevail with:

1. A bright sunlight and clear sky.
2. Sunlight and hazy sky.
3. A cloudy, bright sky.
4. A cloudy, overcast sky.

Each of these light conditions produces a different ratio of highlight and shadow.

Obviously, if we are to produce the best results in outdoor photography, we must, at times, employ some method of reducing the extreme light contrast between the Sun and the sky.

The Reflector

Outdoor lighting contrast can be effectively reduced by the use of an efficient reflecting surface. Although reflectors have been designed and built in various shapes, sizes and materials, the one here described is, for our purposes, a practical means of bouncing the light of the sun or sky into the shadows:

1. Obtain two 1/16 inch thick plywood panels, 24 x 40 inches.
2. Join the panels (on the 40 inch side) with metal strip hinges.
3. Staple, tack, or glue on household aluminum foil which has first been crinkled and then flattened out.
4. Apply one or more coats of flat white paint on the other side of the panels.

Unfolded, the hinged panels furnish a 40 x 48 inch reflecting surface which does not have to be hand held, but can be placed upright at a fixed distance or angle on most supporting surfaces.

Aluminum foil is an efficient reflector and can be used to a distance four times its width.

For a close up shot, use the white side of the reflector. At close range, the white reflector will bounce a soft and uniform light which is less intense than the aluminum foil.

Place the reflector as close to the camera as possible, out of the picture area. Then aim the reflector at the subject. The reflected illumination will readily become apparent. To reduce the intensity of the light, place the reflector farther away from the subject. To increase the intensity of the reflected light, place the reflector closer to the subject.

Figure 158 illustrates a picture that was taken without a reflector.

Figure 159 is the same picture. But here, a reflector was used to open up the shadow areas.

155. An Extreme Light Ratio

156. Over-cast Sky

157. A Well Balanced
     Light Ratio

158. Without a Reflector

159. With a Reflector

Synchro-Sunlight Flash

Another method, and perhaps a more convenient means of changing the outdoor light ratio would be to use flash bulbs or electronic flash as a fill-in illumination.

To achieve a proper balance between the existing natural illumination and the flash:

1. Use a light meter to determine the proper exposure for the existing light alone.
2. Set the camera for the exposure.
3. Determine the flash guide number from flash bulb carton, for the shutter speed for which your camera is set.
4. Divide the guide number by the previously determined lens opening (steps one and two above) to get the subject to flash distance.

Where it is impractical to place the flash at the required footage because of space considerations, such as for a closeup shot, you can reduce the flash intensity by draping a handkerchief across the light reflector.

EQUIPMENT AND ACCESSORIES

In so far as equipment is concerned, we can get along with a minimum: the camera, film, and a light meter. However, a sturdy tripod, a lens shade, a light filter, a reflector or an additional light source (as previously described) can add immeasurably to the quality of the picture taken outdoors.

The Lens Shade

This camera accessory is usually a black lined tube or lens hood (as it is sometimes called) which projects over or around a lens to prevent extraneous light rays from striking the lens. Such rays will set up reflections within the lens, causing optical flare or general fog over the film, thus resulting in reduced contrast on the negative.

The Light Filter

This is a device of colored glass or gelatin which is placed in front of the lens for the purpose of reducing or eliminating the light of some colors, generally those to which the film is most sensitive. However, in specific terms of usage in outdoor photography, filters are employed to dramatize a scene or to otherwise correct it by cutting down the color rays to which the film may be over-sensitive, so that other colors will have time to register. For

152

example, a yellow filter will cut down on the blue and violet light to which most panchromatic films are over-sensitive and register the sky darker, thus producing a contrast or darker tone against which cloud formations will stand out.

However, most filters play havoc with skin tones and therefore should not be used.

The exception to this rule is a light green filter which, when used with panchromatic film, registers the sky or green foliage tones in their true monochromatic values without appreciably changing skin tones.

The Tripod

In simple terms, a tripod is a three-legged stand of metal or wood designed to support a camera during adjustment, framing, and exposure. A good tripod should also be sturdy and steady, have telescoping or adjustable legs to change the camera's elevation, and a properly engineered pan head that allows a good range of vertical and horizontal tilts.

GOING ON LOCATION

Preparation and thorough organization play an important part in making good outdoor photographs. The operation should be planned as carefully as possible. As an example:

1. Select your model and arrange an alternate as a stand-by in the event your model cancels out.
2. Brief the model on your choice of costume elements appropriate to the location setting.
3. Choose the location: seashore, swimming pool, lake, woodland area, state and national parks, etc. If you are not familiar with the location, by all means, make a survey trip. In the event the location is in a restricted area where a permit is required, get it well in advance of shooting time. Most authorities will cooperate with you.
4. A day before the shooting schedule, check weather forecast, wind velocity, and temperature. A model can become quite uncomfortable on a cool or windy day.
5. Check your equipment and see that everything is in good working order.
6. Make a list of everything to be taken on location, and do not skimp on film.
7. Start early enough so you arrive at the location site when the sun is at an angle in the sky. Usually there is about two or three hours of good shooting time. Do not shoot at mid-day when the sun is directly overhead. The sun at this angle produces long vertical shadows and dark eye sockets.

153

Epilogue

AFTER CAREFULLY RE-READING EVERYTHING WRITTEN IN THESE PAGES, I came to the inevitable conclusion that there is no end to learning and teaching. Indeed, it seemed to me that I could keep on writing and illustrating many other facets of this fascinating subject without repeating myself.

However, further thought convinced me that additional treatment in the photography of women would lead me beyond the scope of this book. The fundamental ideas have been covered, so you need only to proceed alone, creating through your own initiative. With this approach, the final results will surely reflect your own creative ability.

And if you make mistakes—write them off to experience from which you will learn to do better. Out of it all will come a desire to investigate, learn further, and develop a style of your own. The point I am trying to make is that the end result is an individual attainment. It is something that every photographer has to work out for himself.

You must, therefore, realize that assimilating the knowledge in this book will not alone open your door to success. The book is meant only to guide you so you can apply the knowledge and form yourself in accordance with your own capabilities.

As a parting thought remember this well: photography is as vast in its scope as the range of the photographer's technical skill, imagination, and inspiration. Though he may never find a face or figure that portrays his ideal, he will always strive to infuse into every photograph some of the beauty he visualizes. This, in essence, is the road to achievement in The photography of women.